# FAVORED
## *From*
# LAST TO FIRST

Authored By
**Kelvin A. Waites Sr.**

*"So the last shall be first, and the first last: for many be called, but few chosen."*

**Matthew 20:16**

PATASKITY PUBLISHING CO.

Pataskity Publishing Co.

207 Hudson Terrace Suite 102

Augusta, GA 30906

pataskitypublishing.com

Copyright © 2024 Kelvin A. Waites Sr.

**All rights reserved.**

No portion of this book may be reproduced mechanically, electronically, or by any other means, including photocopying, without the author's written permission. It is illegal to copy this book, post it on a website, or distribute it by any other means without permission from the author.

# TABLE OF CONTENTS

Introduction: Blessings of the Present ........................................1
Chapter 1: Being Last ................................................................ 6
Chapter 2: Get In the Game ......................................................13
Chapter 3: Facts Change ......................................................... 18
Chapter 4: New Level New Devil ............................................. 25
Chapter 5: In Plain Sight......................................................... 29
Chapter 6: Favor Found Me ..................................................... 39
Chapter 7: Swimming With The Current Purpose And Service 44
Chapter 8: Why Me? ................................................................ 49
Chapter 9: For A Time Such As This....................................... 54
Chapter 10: New Season ......................................................... 69
Chapter 11: First You Too, Can Be First.................................. 74

## WORKBOOK

About Favored From Last To First Workbook ......................... 82
Week One: Based On Chapter One ........................................... 85
Week Two: Based On Chapter Two ...........................................91
Week Three: Based On Chapter Three .................................... 97
Week Four: Based On Chapter Four........................................ 103
Week Five: Based On Chapter Five.......................................... 108
Week Six: Based On Chapter Six ............................................. 114
Week Seven: Based On Chapter Seven .................................... 120
Week Eight: Based On Chapter Eight...................................... 126
Week Nine: Based On Chapter Nine........................................ 131
Week Ten: Based On Chapter Ten ............................................137
Week Eleven: Based On Chapter Eleven ................................. 142
Week Twelve: Based On Poem You Too, Can Be First ...........147

## Introduction
# BLESSINGS OF THE PRESENT

*We are all actors in God's production!*

Do you believe favor is a generational blessing? Take a moment and ponder the concept that blessings, just like rivers, twist and curve through generations. Proverbs 13:22 shares light on this profound truth stating, "A good man leaves an inheritance for his children's children." This wisdom transcends the mere accumulation of wealth, both material and spiritual, prosperity, and a legacy of greatness awaiting for the lives of generations yet unborn. My journey, stitched with memories of my upbringing, echoes the resounding impact of my descendants' wisdom and choices. Through their lives, a legacy of favor and integrity was meticulously crafted and passed down.

At the heart of this legacy stood my father, Isaac Waites, a beacon of virtue whose life's blueprint had an astounding impact on me and aided in shaping my path. With roots deep in the soil of Johns Island, South Carolina, his early years were marked by tragedy, hardship, and resilience. Despite the challenges, including a devastating house fire, Isaac's spirit remained unbroken, embarking on a lifetime of hard work from the tender age of twelve. His guiding principles were simple yet profound: Trust in God, work hard, and live in service to others. *"We are all actors in God's production,"* he would often remind us, emphasizing our collective role in the divine play of life. Isaac's wisdom, a testament to his character, shined brightly despite his modest educational background, teaching us the true essence of success and fulfillment.

Even though my father's formal education was interrupted after his completion of the sixth grade, he was one of the smartest human beings I have ever known. The essence of his wisdom, strength, and grit was he chose his words carefully, and only spoke when he had something of substance to share. Isaac's narrative was further distinguished by a unique medical condition, Situs Inversus, where his internal organs lay in a mirror image of their typical arrangement. In other words, his heart was positioned on the right side of his body, instead of the left. Situs Inversus affects about 1 in every 10,000 people. This rare genetic twist, discovered only as his health began to wane, added a layer of mystique to his already remarkable existence, underscoring the profound uniqueness each of us carries within. Isaac Waites was a unique human being in so many ways.

Parallel to Isaac's resilience, my mother, Frances, had unwavering faith, and her spirit was as deep and nurturing as her Gullah Geechee roots. Despite the gaps in her formal education, her wisdom and fortitude were boundless, instilling in me a sense of confidence and self-assuredness from my earliest days. She would tell me from the time in her deep Gullah Geechee voice, *"Momma say, I been born with the veil over my eyes, and ain't nobody gonna ever be able to fool me."* It was not until I was an adult that I realized what she meant was she had an en caul birth. An en caul birth is an incredibly rare event where a baby is born encased in their amniotic sac. When a baby is *"born inside of a veil"* it looks as if the baby is born in a thin sac with amniotic fluid in it. Some people believe there is a spiritual meaning to a baby being born en caul since such births are rare. Many cultures, including my own, view it as a mark of protection, blessing, or prophecy. It is believed being born *"with a veil"* means the baby will be protected or achieve greatness. An en caul birth symbolizes a special destiny. It carries spiritual meaning, with the child marked for a unique path in life. My mother's discernment as a result of her en caul birth, was a beacon of guiding light, as her words and wisdom proved to be true.

My mother's grandmother, who she called *"Momma",* was Elizabeth Roper, and she lived downtown Charleston, South Carolina, near the back gate of the Citadel Military College. Elizabeth Roper, a matriarch whose essence was the epitome of Gullah Geechee strength and wisdom. Her home in Charleston was not only a dwelling place, but also a sanctuary where love, faith, and cultural pride intertwined seamlessly. Elizabeth's legacy was vividly captured in her creation of quilts—each stitch a testament to community, resilience, and care—and in the sacred rituals of her kitchen.

My mom really looked up to and worshiped the ground my great grandmother walked on. Until this day, it is common for her to start off a sentence with *"Momma say."* Having a Gullah Geechee family culture played a major role in our faith as well. While we did not have much materistically, love and our faith accommodated everything else. I recall the pride and conviction my great grandmother spoke with, and the attention and respect she demanded when she was holding court. She would often make handmade quilts, and give them to family, friends, or whoever needed them in the community. When all of the family from across the country would come to Charleston, everyone would visit and reside at her home. She was loving and made everyone feel welcome.

I remember her house being beautiful with hardwood floors, and the walls covered with her love and comfort. Some of the Gullah Geechee style meals she made, which all had a prerequisite of a fresh pot of white rice, were lima beans with any and every part of the pig in it, okra soup with tomatoes and corn, shrimp and grits, and she would make and amazing bread pudding. One of my most cherished memories involves Elizabeth, enveloped in the warmth of her kitchen, crafting bread pudding with an air of reverence and tradition. As she delicately tore the "jokers"—the end pieces of the loaf—her voice would rise in the melodies of old Negro spirituals, each note a thread connecting us to the past and future. *"This is the day, this is the day that the Lord has made, I will rejoice and be glad in it"* she sang, her voice a blend of hope, history, and strength. In these moments, as the scent of cinnamon and sugar filled the air, I experienced the tangible presence of our ancestors, each song a bridge to the lessons and legacies of those who walked before us.

I would not trade the Gullah Geechee culture and my upbringing for anything. I learned so many lessons about life from the older folks in my family, and in the community. These roots, deep and nourishing, have imbued in me lessons of life that resonate with the wisdom of ages. From the profound simplicity of *"Manners will take you places that money can't,"* to the foundational truth that *"Charity begins at home,"* the voices of my ancestors continue to guide and inspire me. This rich inheritance, a mosaic of faith, resilience, and love, is a legacy I cherish deeply. In embracing the gifts of my heritage, I find myself woven into a story much larger than my own—a story of grace, perseverance, and the enduring light of hope.

# Chapter 1

# BEING LAST

*I recognize the journey to success is not found in shortcuts, but in the steadfast climb, step by step, with courage and determination shaping my destiny.*

Growing up in Harlem, New York, with my family and older brother, Bryan, poverty was our silent companion, though its presence barely registered through our youthful ignorance. We lived on the fourteenth floor of the projects, in a modest two-bedroom apartment we affectionately termed our "penthouse." This was no ordinary penthouse but a haven where dreams, as vast as the view of Yankee Stadium's glowing lights, felt both close yet impossibly distant. Our parents worked extremely hard but every red penny went towards keeping the *"Waites ship"* afloat, by providing our basic needs, which were food in our stomachs, clothes on our backs, and shelter over our heads.

Indeed, I referred to our home as a penthouse with intent, not irony. Our top-floor apartment afforded us a view that Bryan and I cherished, even if it only offered a visual, not physical, escape from our reality. Amidst this backdrop, Bryan would mimic Howard Cossell, bringing to life imaginary baseball games, because we knew it was far-fetched to believe we would ever attend a live game in person. Howard Cossell was a legendary sports commentator and media personality that gained fame from his relationship and coverage of Muhamad Ali. Our imaginary games were unique – the players were the rats and the roaches that shared our home. This, to us, was normal, the only entertainment we needed.

While Bryan and I did not have a full understanding of how sad it was to imagine a game between the rats and the roaches at the time, my brother and I thrived on imagination, our bond, and the unwavering love within our family. Our parents, embodying the epitome of hard work, dedicated every ounce of their energy to provide for us, ensuring we never lacked the essentials. We had Christian parents who worked around the clock. My dad was a mechanic by trade, and my mom worked at the phone company and Beekman Hospital. We were what was called *"latchkey kids"* at the time because most days after school we were unsupervised and cared for ourselves. Our adventures extended beyond the confines of our apartment, turning the streets of Harlem into a playground of endless possibilities. We fancied ourselves as the urban equivalents of Tom Sawyer and Huckleberry Finn, with each day presenting a new adventure.

Some evenings were spent at Grandmother Viola's in the Bronx. She was a God fearing woman, and taught us how to pray. Her lessons in faith, particularly the 23rd Psalm, and her unique bedtime rituals, added layers of warmth and protection to our lives, even if it meant being swaddled so tightly we could barely move. She taught us how to recite Psalm 23, and would tell us not to worry if we could not remember it in its entirety. She said in that case in any situation to just say *"The Lord is my Shepherd, I shall not want."* She believed in the Golden Rule, and overall being a good person. I remember her tucking us in at night. This was not a traditional T.V, or story book kind of tucking in where you would give a kid a warm stuffed animal, kiss him or her on the forehead, and tell them, *"goodnight."* My grandmother would tuck us in by tucking the quilt, and the sheet tightly between the mattress and the box spring, so tight it was hard to move once we were in the bed under the covers. I thought to myself, *"We are wrapped up and tucked in so tight, we felt like mummies, and she still wants us to recite the 23 Psalm."* The pressure from the quilt being tucked so tight left us out of breath most nights before we finished. I often found humor in the situation as I fell to sleep.

She would also put cotton in our ears and our noses. As a child, I never understood why, but I later learned it was to keep insects from crawling in the openings of our bodies while we were asleep. I remember her saying, *"if you feel something on the foot of the bed, just shake your feet and they will go away."* *"They"* were the rats that frequented her apartment building. My grandmother was a stickler for cleanliness, and kept an extremely clean house, but her apartment building was infested with rats just like most of New York City was at the time. Outside of the challenges of poverty, we were close knit, loved one another, and were taught that God was our provider.

Yet, my childhood wasn't devoid of challenges. Crooked legs necessitated years in braces, making me an easy target for bullies and casting a shadow over my self-esteem. Asthma added to my trials, with frequent emergency room visits marking my early years. The slightest amount of any dust particles would trigger violent asthma attacks. Inhalers and other medications did not do me any justice, so my family and I spent several hours on many occasions in the hospital, waiting to see a doctor to get the shots that would get my asthma under control. It was not apparent to me as a child but most of the time we spent waiting was due to the fact that we did not have insurance and the local hospitals focused their efforts on people who did first. As a result of my circumstances, I did not think my life would ever amount to anything because these health conditions had a negative affect on my self-esteem, and I knew exactly how it felt to feel hopeless. Looking back, hopelessness equated to having to wait at the back of the line. Hopelessness engulfed me like a dark room that I was in, and unable to find the light switch. Ultimately, hopelessness was even when I found the light switch and clicked it on either there was no power or no light bulb to show me the way out. These experiences, though painful, taught me resilience and gave me a unique perspective on hope and perseverance.

The highlight of my day was whether or not the elevator in our building was working. Life's daily climb, literal and metaphorical, was embodied in our journey to and from our apartment. If it was working, I would be thankful, but If not, which was often, Bryan and I faced the stairs, a daunting endeavor exacerbated by my physical conditions. My legs would cramp up, and sometimes I would even have asthma attacks right there in the stairwell! I remember seeing people in the stairwell having sex, using drugs, urinating or defecating, and many other activities. Bryan would encourage me, and say, *"Come on man, keep moving!"* He would say, *"If you stop, it is going to get harder!"* Sometimes if the elevator did work, it would go as far as the sixth, seventh, or eighth floor, but no higher.

When that occurred, Bryan would climb to the top of the elevator, pull me out, and we would go to the next floor. This was normal for us as kids! It was always something going on, and we never realized how much danger we were in on a daily basis! We could have been killed if the elevator moved while we were climbing from floor to floor. I do not share this story for sympathy, but this experience taught me a very important lesson about life. That lesson is, *"There is no magical elevator that will come along to take us to any level of success. We all have to walk up the steps."*

During this time, Bryan and I attended a Catholic school called St. Aloysius in Harlem. One of the coolest things I remember about St. Aloysius was how diverse it was. There were so many different races and nationalities represented amongst my classmates. Everyone got along because we all respected and embraced our differences. If any of us forgot we were all human beings, the Nuns would touch the palm of our hands with their wooden rulers and remind us. Attending this school was an early lesson in life for me, and would shape how I saw the world as an adult. How could children from different cultures and walks of life figure things out and learn how to work together for the benefit of everyone? It was simple: *"It started and ended with our leadership."*

I would see so much crime as we traveled back and forth from school. Everything from armed robbery, people being beaten in the streets with baseball bats and urinated on in broad daylight. I cannot begin to tell you how rough Harlem was during that time. It was pretty terrifying and it was a trauma we could not erase from our minds. I knew my parents wanted to get us out of the city, but they did not have the money or the resources to do it at the time.

I recall an incident when Bryan and I were walking home one day from school; we realized a guy was following us. *"The shaggy man,"* is what we called him when we look back on what happened. He was a scruffy and shaggy image of a shadow from what I remember. Once we realized he was following us, we began to walk faster and faster. As we started to get close to home, we could only hope the elevator was working; however, the *"Out of Order"* sign was on the elevator. This was bad because we immediately knew we had to walk up the steps. Bryan could actually run, but there was no way he would run and leave me, as I could not run due to the leg braces I was confined to at the time. As we were walking as quickly as we could, we could look down and see he was still following us. He was getting close and we were terrified! He kept getting closer and closer, while never saying a word. We could hear him grunting and breathing hard, as if the steep climb of the steps was challenging physically. I'm not sure if it was my imagination triggered by fear, but it really sounded like something that was not human chasing us.

My brother and I finally made it up all fourteen flights of steps to our apartment. He took out his key, and we made it inside. We thought we were homefree, but the *"Shaggy Man"* stuck his arm in the door at the last minute. I held the door until my brother came back from getting something to hit the *"Shaggy Man's"* hand. I know I was only holding the door for about ten seconds but at the time it seemed like an eternity. Till this day, I do not know how I held the door, and kept this intruder from getting in, because I was a short chubby kid, and did not have one ounce of athleticism in me.

Our encounter with the "Shaggy Man," a frightening chase up fourteen flights of stairs, highlighted the stark realities of our environment and ultimately, spurred our family's move to Charleston, South Carolina. This move was a pivotal moment, marking the beginning of a new chapter away from the hardships of Harlem.

Reflecting on my upbringing, I recognize the invaluable lessons learned in the diverse halls of St. Aloysius Catholic School, where diversity was celebrated and respect for all was paramount. The challenges we faced, from poverty to personal trials, shaped my worldview, teaching me that success is not about finding shortcuts but embracing the climb, step by step, with faith and determination.

## Chapter 2
# GET IN THE GAME

*I embrace new beginnings and challenges as opportunities to grow, proving to myself that with resilience and determination, I can adapt and thrive in any environment.*

In Charleston, South Carolina, we moved into a modest, three-bedroom brick house in a quiet neighborhood in the West Ashley section of Charleston. It was a stressful transition for the entire family. Both of my parents were looking for work, and things were not moving as fast as they anticipated. They had a little bit of money they saved for a rainy day, but since we moved to South Carolina it seemed like it was raining every day.

I previously imagined our move from Harlem to Charleston would be an exciting fresh start. After all, I was able to escape the challenges my family and I faced up North. Yet, it introduced a different set of challenges. My Northern accent and neatly pressed clothes set me apart, making it hard to blend in. My attempts to connect were met with ridicule; my differences were not celebrated but scorned.

The neighborhood kids made fun of me on a daily basis, so I pretty much stayed to myself. I was on the tail end of having to wear leg braces, and due to my asthma, even though my breathing was better, I did not quite have the confidence to do what other kids were doing. I tried really hard to fit in, but nothing I did was good enough, or made me more likable by my peers. Lack of confidence and self-esteem were major challenges for me. I was doing better physically, but it seemed mentally like I was far behind and trying to play catch up.

Out of all the kids in the neighborhood, I was only able to make one friend; his name was John and he was Caucasian kid that lived in my neighborhood around the corner. Despite being different races and from different cultures, John and I were genuine friends. We became best friends and embraced each other. During those days, we did not have the technology as kids have today. After school, John and I would spend hours riding bikes. We caught dragonflies by the tail with sewing thread. Because we were friends, I was called, *"cracker lover,"* and he was called *"nigger lover."* It just did not seem fair as we were just kids, and I was not acquainted with racism due to it not being as prevalent in New York. I thought to myself, *"They do not want to be my friend, but they are criticizing me over the only friend I have."* Becoming acclimated to my new surroundings in South Carolina had its fair share of challenges!

I felt as if I had swapped one group of problems for a new set of problems. Even though I was trying I just did not fit in with my peers. I felt like I was shunned and put on an island by myself because I was different. The kids in the neighborhood not only ridiculed me, but my father was also skeptical of my friendship with John. Although my dad was a Christian, he questioned our friendship, and I struggled with that. I recall my dad saying, *"I want you to be careful with your friend."* I was confused by the fact that my dad was telling me one thing, and it did not line up with the friendship I established with John. My dad said to me, *"When push comes to shove, they gonna be pushing and you gonna get shoved."* I do not think my father was trying to transfer his biased beliefs towards me; instead, he was trying to protect me because he had seen so much hatred. Dad grew up in the South during the 1940's when segregation, Jim Crow Laws, and racism was at its peak. He did not want me to be harmed, so he warned me. I walked away from my dad feeling confused. He ultimately meant that when times got tough, white people would stick together, and black people would always get the short end of the stick.

My parents never placed any pressure on me, but I pressured myself to get acclimated to life in the South. I knew both of my parents sacrificed their careers, leaving their jobs, borrowed money, and moved my brother and I in hopes we will have better lives. I could not watch them make such sacrifices, and allow the problems I faced to keep me from making the best out of our new life in South Carolina. I knew I had to get with it! I needed to make a change to survive in the South; I had to get in the game. A change was needed and a change was made! I got in the game because I evolved as a person.

I was starting to figure out I was pretty athletic, and I wanted to play organized football really bad. I asked my parents but they would not let me, because they felt that I was just too fragile. I watched some of the other kids in the neighborhood come, and go wearing their football equipment, but I knew at least this particular year, I was not going to play.

I begged my parents all summer to let me play organized football at the beginning of the next football season. My mom really did not want to let me play, and had no desire to change her mind. My father spoke with my mother, and told her they needed to give me a chance because it sounded like something I really wanted to do. My mom reluctantly agreed to let me play organized football at St. Andrews Parks and Playgrounds.

Based on the fact that I was about ten years old, and had a pretty solid stature, I was selected to play on a team in the Small Fry League. I was not only excited about my first practice, but also nervous at the same time! Most of the other kids had a couple of years of experience under their belts, and this was my first ride with the rodeo. My father knew he had to get off from work early to make sure I made it to my very first practice on time. When my father turned the corner, he could see me waiting at the head of the driveway with my football uniform on, and my helmet in my hand.

I got in the car with my dad, and off we went to the football field. Once we arrived at the football field, dad got out of the car but I did not. I was like a kid being dropped off at school for the first time. My father walked around to the passenger side window, and said to me, "Kelvin, you can do this, just believe in yourself." I got out of the car, and walked over to the football field with my father. I did not know it then, but my father was just as scared, if not more, than I was. On the walk from the car to the football field, I could only imagine one thousand thoughts ran through my dad's mind. I am sure he thought about how I had battled crooked legs, and how I had to wear the leg braces. He thought about how I suffered from asthma, and questioned whether or not I would even be able to effectively play football. He thought about how I had been bullied, and my confidence level never being where it really needed to be. My father also thought about the fact that he knew absolutely nothing about the game of football. He didn't know the difference between a quarterback and a wide receiver. He was not athletic, and never played any sports because his childhood was cut short. My dad felt helpless because I was about to embark on a new journey in my life, and he did not know what to tell me or how to help me.

When we made it to the football field, I looked up at my dad for instructions, not realizing that he did not know what to say. I believed in my dad, and was willing to do whatever my father told me to do. What he said to me would in so many words release me from any limitations I may have ever put on myself. It awakened and freed me. What my father said to me next would change my life. The only thing he knew to tell me was, *"HIT 'EM BEFORE THEY HIT YOU."* It was like what he said set me free. Nothing that happened prior to that moment mattered anymore. I started playing football on that day, and did exactly what my father told me to do. During my first football season ever, I played running back and linebacker, and was selected as an all-star most valuable player for my football team. I was labeled as the hardest worker and hardest hitter on my team. What my father told me that day forever changed my life! It was not just about football, but it was also about life.

## Chapter 3

# FACTS CHANGE

*I recognize my worth and embrace my journey, knowing my struggles are part of my story, leading me to true strength and resilience.*

For once, I did not feel like I was trailing behind everyone else. After my successful football season and earning the title of "Most Valuable Player," I experienced a fleeting moment of significance. However, the familiar, undermining voice inside me persisted, suggesting my achievements were just a stroke of luck, branding me an imposter destined to be exposed. This internal adversary highlighted my flaws: my crooked legs, my asthma, my humble beginnings in Harlem, convincing me I was undeserving of success, happiness, or recognition. Why was it so hard to silence that voice and accept my hard-earned victory on the football field?

The strangest thing was kids who never supported or wanted to be friends with me all of a sudden had a change of heart. On one hand it felt like over night they gained enough respect for me to finally *"SEE"* and accept me in their circles, but I knew it was not real. It is intriguing how human beings flock to and have a desire to align themselves with individuals or teams that they deem winners or successful. Even though everyone wanted to be friends with me, I still felt lonely, isolated, and not worthy because they had no idea who I was. It is so ironic how people see what they believe is your "GlORY," but they know absolutely nothing about your "STORY." In other words, people see you win or prosper, but they have no idea what you had to endure in order to even make it to that point.

My excellence in sports, especially football, became a constructive outlet for the anger, frustration, and aggression that had accumulated over the years, as a result of my physical limitations, socio-economic status, and my low self-esteem. For the first time, I tasted what *"hope"* felt like, and its flavor was intoxicating, though I was unsure how to continue savoring it.

Even after my dad warned me, and planted seeds of doubt about him, John and I continued to be friends. We eventually drifted apart, each finding our own path. He delved into music, discovering his talent in playing instruments and singing. Our casual encounters were friendly, yet we both knew we were on different journeys now. Alone again, I felt isolated, as if stranded on an island where no one spoke my language or cared to understand me. This period was one of the most formative times of my life.

During this isolating time, I found solace with my Aunt Ada, a wise and grounded presence in my life. Her Gullah Geechee heritage and deep accent provided me with a connection to my roots I had missed out on growing up in Harlem. She lived in the Housing Authority on King Street in downtown Charleston, and I spent a lot of time with her helping her out around her house.

I would cut her grass, clean windows, or do any other odd jobs she came up with for me to do. Honestly, I had what was called an *"old soul"* and actually enjoyed being around and listening to older folks. Aunt Ada was Gullah Geechee to her core, and I could listen to her talk all day long. Spending the first ten years of my life in Harlem, deprived me of having the opportunity of developing a full Gullah Geechee accent. Aunt Ada's accent was so deep she pronounced my name as Cabin (like log Cabin), instead of Kelvin. She would always say *"look yeah, here me wha I say; Cabin you gon be somebody one day. You here wha I say? The 'debil (devil) gonna try you, but all you got to do is trust God and stay 'umble (humble)."* During the course of the day, she would pack her pipe with Granger tobacco, and I couldn't wait for her to light it up in the evening because I loved the way it smelled.

Aunt Ada spoke positivity, hope, and life into me at a time in my life when I needed it most, and I will never forget her for that. One of my fondest memories of Aunt Ada was the conversations she would have with various church members after church on Sunday afternoons. I would act like I was watching television or occupied, but trust and believe, I was listening. Man, they would say some things! One day, I remember she was talking about a church member who had unexpectedly passed away. They were trying to make sense of it, and I remember like yesterday Aunt Ada's take on the situation. She said *"see yeah, when da secretary call yo name, you gots to answer. That's why we gots to work while it's daylight cuz darkness shall come."* In other words, when God says it is your time, you have to go, and that is why it is important to do what you can while you can. Those comments always stuck with me!

I was always respectful to Aunt Ada saying *"yes ma'am or no ma'am,"* but deep down on my insides, I would think to myself *"either this old lady is crazy or she really believed in me."* God called her name many years ago, but I could never forget everything she did for me. She had more wit, and wisdom than I can ever imagine having.

My journey also included regular church attendance mandated by my parents. They required Bryan and I to attend church on a regular basis, sometimes three and four times a week. They believed Bryan and I were two young black boys from Harlem, who would face countless struggles, barriers, and in some cases would have to run twice as fast as other kids in order to be successful in life. Knowing this, they realized we needed to have a personal relationship with God, and understand the sacrifice he made in sending his son Jesus to save the world.

I realize today my parents wanted to do their part in preparing us for the ups and downs of life, but to be totally honest, at that point in my life, I hated going to church. I was like most twelve year old boys who just wanted to hang out, play video games, and not take life too seriously. The more we went to church, the more I resented my parents for making me go. My dad would often take us to Sunday school, and he would return home. My parents always made sure we had some change for Sunday school. Sometimes they gave us twenty-five cents, and other times they gave us fifty. I never felt like anyone would notice if I left Sunday School, so I would go missing. As some kids would cut regular school, I was a master at cutting Sunday school. As soon as my dad left, I would go to Ladson's Corner Store located on the corner of Kennedy and President Streets in downtown Charleston, to spend my Sunday school money on candy. I had lots of fun choosing which candies to buy. The store sold *Lemon-Heads*, *Boston Baked Beans*, and my favorite was *Now and Later*. Back then, fifty cents would go a long way.

My routine came to an abrupt end one day when the Sunday school superintendent shared with my parents that my brother always had his money, but I never had mine. One Sunday morning, my father pretended to leave like he always did. He drove around the block like he was leaving, but he came back to the store, and I was busted. My scheme was over! The day my father caught me cutting Sunday School was the last time I went back to the Ladson Corner Store! During the church service, people thought I was up clapping, praising God, and shouting Hallelujah because I was into the service, but they did not realize, I was uncomfortable sitting down because my backside was on fire! I thought to myself on many occasions, *"I cannot wait to grow up and get out of this house,"* because I wanted to do what Kelvin Waites wanted to do. Unfortunately, going to church was not one of the things at the top of my list.

Like many other times before my mom told me she would be attending a week long revival service at Bible Way Baptist Church on Savage Road in Charleston. I remember her saying *"You don't have to go every night, but I do expect you to go at least one night."* The only good thing about it, if there was such a thing, was out of the kindness of her heart, she allowed me to pick the night I would attend.

I was not looking forward to it, but I remember that night like it was yesterday. I was so angry I had to go, and looking back my heart was not in the right place to receive a word from God, let alone anyone else. The church was packed, and I sat as far in the back, and as close to the door as I possibly could. I did not know what a cell phone was at the time, but I imagine today, if I had one or some type of gaming system either one would have occupied my mind during the revival service. I remember

Reverend Randolph Miller, who later became a popular TV personality, was preaching this particular night. The choir was singing like they were trying to wake the dead, and I remember the Pastor preaching so hard he was profusely sweating. The church was truly on fire for the Lord that night.

I was reluctantly present that night, sitting in the back, closed off to the message being shared. For the life of me, I could not understand why I was so angry! I believe it was because my mom was asking me to believe in something or someone I could not even see. Hell, I didn't even believe in myself, so it was a hard sell to ask me to praise and worship God and believe in miracles, especially when I myself was hopeless. Yet, something profound happened. Overwhelmed by an inexplicable force, I found myself weeping uncontrollably. Before I realized what was happening, I was being guided to the front of the church, by an usher to the section up front on the left side of the pulpit, also known as the *"Amen corner."* While sitting there, doing my best to understand what was happening, and trying to gain my composure, Reverend Miller appeared with a microphone in his hand. As he walked towards me, the choir was singing, the Deacons were praying, and the church was shouting and praising *their Lord.* When he reached me, he thrust the microphone in front of me and asked me one question. It seemed as if time froze and you could literally hear a needle drop. He asked, *"son, why are you crying?"* I was speechless, and in that moment of vulnerability, confronted by Reverend Miller, I could only express that I felt touched by an unseen presence. All I could say was, *"I felt like something touched me."* When I was sitting in the back row, angry, and talking at the same time it felt like someone walked up behind me and grabbed me by both shoulders and shook me up. The odd thing was when I looked back nobody was there. At that moment, I was afraid more than anything else. When the congregation of about one hundred and twenty people heard what I said, the entire church erupted with a loud roar, praise, and rejoiced like their favorite team had just scored a touchdown during the Super Bowl. That night, amidst my confusion and fear, I experienced a divine revelation, leading me to accept Jesus Christ as my Savior. It was a pivotal moment, marking the beginning of a new chapter in my life, one where I started to understand the importance of faith and the role it would play in shaping my future.

# Chapter 4
# NEW LEVEL NEW DEVIL

*I trust in the journey and embrace my unique path, knowing each challenge I face is a divine opportunity to strengthen my faith and demonstrate resilience.*

Just like many young Christians struggle along their journey, my journey was no different. Embracing my faith didn't shield me from struggles; if anything, it added a complex layer to my adolescence. I was about to become a teenager, my hormones were all over the place, and I thought I had it all figured out. I also struggled being a boy who accepted Christ as my personal Savior. As I navigated the tumult of teenage years, I found it challenging to wear my faith openly, especially around my football teammates and peers. Admitting my beliefs felt like revealing a weakness, a misconception that masked the true courage and strength it takes to stand firm in one's faith. I was ignorant of the many stories in the Bible of men who believed with conviction in God, and were willing to lay it all on the line in the name of the Lord. There's nothing weak or soft about that!

After my spiritual awakening at Bible Way, my life ironically enough seemed to be just a bit tougher. What should have been a blessing almost seemed to be a curse. I experienced a new level of spiritually, and along with that came a new set of problems.

To be totally honest and transparent, I was living a double life. I ping-ponged back and forth between two worlds: the tough, unyielding persona I adopted for my school and neighborhood, and the devout, faithful front I maintained at home and church. I played along acting like I was all in with the Jesus thing, even though I really was not. *Besides, why would God love me?* I had asthma, crooked legs, was poor, I was not the best student, I was short and husky, dark skinned, and did not even like myself. I wrestled with the notion of God's love for someone as seemingly inconsequential as me. It was hard living two lives, but I did not have a choice.

If that wasn't bad enough, peculiar things started happening. I started having weird dreams, and shortly thereafter, something would happen in real life. I recall once having a dream I was walking while holding someone's hand. In the dream I could not see who was holding my hand, but we were walking up the steps of the church we attended in Harlem. I could tell it was some type of procession because the ushers were positioned on both sides as we entered the church wearing black suits and dresses, and they all had on white gloves. It was obvious to me that we were attending someone's funeral.

In my dream, we continued walking and finally reached the entrance of the church. At that point, I was able to see a casket at the very front of the church. It looked like it was three miles away and it seemed to be the longest walk from the entrance to the front of the church. We kept walking until we made it to the casket and I was finally able to see who was inside. When I looked in the casket, I was shocked, confused, and frightened all at the same time. I saw my father lying in the casket as if he was sleeping. I was even more taken aback when my dream finally allowed me to look to the left, and discover who I was walking and holding hands with the entire time.

Surprisingly enough it was my father. I took several double takes from the casket to the person holding my hand, almost feeling like I was watching a tennis match thinking; *"How could my dad be in the casket sleeping, and be walking beside me holding my hand at the same time?"* I woke up from the dream terrified and confused. I was terribly upset at the thought of my dad being dead in that casket when I knew he was still alive, and bewildered as to how he could be in two places at one time. I frantically ran to my mother's room to tell her what I saw, but she didn't react the way I thought she would. Honestly, she didn't react at all. She was very calm and did not seem bothered, or surprised by what I was telling her.

My mom sat me down and calmly told me, *"Kelvin, you are favored and God has given you a very special gift."* She said it was only the beginning and it wasn't something I should be afraid of. She told me that I had God's anointing, and he had a CALLING on my life. Momma said, *"Now that you have seen the dream, your job is to watch as well as pray."* What she meant was that I needed to pay close attention to my surroundings, and pray to God that he would reveal whatever I saw in my dream. Following this revelation, my dreams took on a new significance. When Uncle Mossa, my father's beloved uncle, passed away shortly after my dream, it was clear my visions were not mere coincidences but a divine warning system. I learned to journal these dreams, capturing their essence upon waking, acknowledging this gift that set me apart.

This gift has guided me my entire life, but I've never really openly talked about it except to my closest family members. This gift, however, felt more like a burden, especially as it cast me further into isolation among my relatives, many of whom feared becoming the subject of my prophetic dreams. This alienation did little for my already wavering self-esteem and posed new questions about my faith: *Why would God entrust such a heavy responsibility to me?* I always felt below the surface that the pattern of my life was *"Two steps forward, and three steps back."*

The *"new devil"* in my life was not an external adversary, but the persistent, negative voice in my head constantly undermining my worth and achievements. This voice was a relentless critic, sowing seeds of doubt and fear. Yet, the journey taught me an invaluable lesson: the power of faith equity. This concept—understanding that past trials and God's unwavering support are testaments to His enduring presence—became my stronghold. Through every challenge, I learned that reinforcing my faith with the memories of God's previous interventions empowered me to face new obstacles with confidence. This belief, that God who guided me before would do so again, became my foundation, transforming each roadblock into a stepping stone towards greater spiritual maturity.

## Chapter 5

# IN PLAIN SIGHT

*I trust my unique talents and genuine self will guide me to my rightful place, and I embrace each step of my journey with confidence and faith in my eventual success.*

Despite my talent on the football field, my academic performance in middle and high school was less than stellar, primarily because I did just enough to scrape by. This attitude stemmed from feeling invisible, a sensation that strangely comforted me, as it meant avoiding additional attention for any reason, including academic achievements. This mindset prevented me from grasping how academics could empower my aspirations, both on the field and in future career choices.

The sad thing was I did not have anyone to push me. My parents, who had not finished high school themselves, were caught up in a cycle of hard work just to keep us afloat, leaving little time for educational support. Our life was a routine of work, church, and the occasional Sunday dinner, devoid of leisure activities or vacations. This isn't a critique of my parents but an acknowledgment of our reality. Despite our move from Harlem, our financial struggles persisted, epitomized by my mother's saying, "*A stomach full is a stomach full,*" which underscored our focus on basic survival over culinary delights. I watched and listened to other kids around me talk about their families; I was amazed at some of the stories they told about family outings, whether it was a nice restaurant or a vacation. I often dreamed about doing some of the cool things with my family other kids were doing with their families.

Even though my family moved from Harlem, our socio-economic situation did not change. We were still poor, living paycheck to paycheck, and while Bryan and I slept at night, I could imagine my parents were up trying to figure out how to *"rob Peter to pay Paul;"* however, my parents worked extremely hard to make sure we had a shelter over our heads and food in our stomachs.

In high school, football became my refuge, the one place where I felt a sense of belonging. I was definitely an introvert; I felt more comfortable staying to myself in my own world. Ironically enough, one major reason I stayed away from people was because I did not want to be in a position where I had to look them in their eyes to communicate. For some reason, during this season in my life, I always believed if someone looked me in my eyes, it would allow them to look into the window of my soul; I did not believe people would like all of the ugly things I went through and they would instantly judge me. This was not true, and I was not aware at the time Satan was an opposer whose job was to make me think the opposite of my reality, and steal any glimpse of hope I may have. This isolation made me a target for local gangs and groups, though I never aligned myself with any, lacking the street credibility that might have offered some protection. Yet, my father's advice to stand firm and think independently was a guiding principle.

My performance on the field improved significantly in my junior and senior years, driven by my determination to join the U.S. Air Force post-graduation, seeking a better life beyond the confines of my current environment. While I did not fit in with any particular group outside of football, I felt safe on the team. We all had something in common. We wanted to win and did not mind working hard to make it happen. I still used football as an outlet to funnel the frustrations of my life, often hitting or tackling someone so hard I would sometimes hurt myself. I was known as one of the hardest hitting defensive backs in our region.

Surprisingly, my football skills attracted college recruiters. While I was not the biggest, fastest, or strongest, I had good instincts and played with force and aggression. I honestly would sacrifice my body while playing without any thought of potentially hurting myself.

I started getting recruiting letters from various schools like Clemson, University of South Carolina, The Citadel, North Carolina State, and Presbyterian College, just to name a few. The letters would go directly to my coaches and they would then pass them on to me. I initially concealed the potential opportunities from my parents, fearing the pressure to pursue an academic path I was not interested in. I just wanted to get my life started. As time went on, it became more difficult to hide from my parents the fact I was being recruited by colleges to play football because my high school coaches were now communicating with them.

The last thing I wanted to do was go to college even though my mom was intrigued with the idea of someone in her family getting a college education knowing that she and my dad never had that opportunity. She did not want me anywhere near the military because it was hard on my family when my older brother Bryan joined the U.S. Navy. Two weeks after Bryan graduated from high school, he left for his initial training with the Navy. I remember the empty feeling I felt when he left. He was my best friend, and had always been there for me. After his secondary training, off to the Persian Gulf he went. It was hard on my family not hearing from Bryan for weeks at a time, and not knowing if he was dead or alive. Even though I had no desire to go to college, it hurt me to see my family on pins and needles constantly worrying about him.

Eventually, my secret came out, leading to my reluctant commitment to Newberry College. My mother along with my entire family was happy, proud, and excited. I was pursuing a college education, and would be continuing my football career at a different level. I was a nervous wreck going to college. I knew it was a new start academically as well as on the football field. Other than the coaches who recruited me, no one knew who Kelvin Waites was. In addition to this new start in my life, I still was not connected to the feeling of belonging; I did not feel I was good enough, or deserved to be there.

I showed up on Newberry College's campus during the hottest part of August and it was game on. Football camp started one month before regular students were scheduled to arrive on campus. I was not prepared mentally or physically for what I was about to face. I had never worked as hard as I did that summer in my life. During my high school years, I skated by doing the bare minimum in the class and the weight room. In high school, my accomplishments on the football field were based on my raw athletic ability and will to win.

I was a new student athlete, green, and unaware of the hard work required to compete on that level. The truth was everyone had raw talent. Each athlete was big, strong and fast. What you did in addition to your raw talent is what made the difference! In other words, my success would be determined by many things such as how much I studied my playbook and my opponent, how hard I worked in the weightroom to get stronger, and my willingness to sacrifice for the team. This experience took me back to my childhood as it reminded me of the stairways in our apartment complex. I learned early in life that no magical elevator was going to pick me up and take me where I needed to go. I knew if I was going to be a successful student athlete, I would have to *walk up the steps or go home*. Many of my negative experiences became foundational lessons to me creating my success. They became my motivation.

Nobody knew who I was. You must understand in most cases when a new player enters the collegiate level, it does not matter how good you were in high school. It is like playing little league all over again because you have to fight to even be seen by your teammates and coaches. Considering this, I was already at a disadvantage because I was not used to the demands of being a college athlete. Whenever you play college football or any other college sport, it becomes your life. Weightroom at five in the morning, meetings throughout the day, practice, more meetings, and then study hall until about ten at night. For a freshman, it is almost impossible to grasp all of that and be able to go out and perform; whereas, the upperclassmen were acclimated to that environment. I played cornerback in high school, but got bigger over the summer and I was moved to strong safety in college. The fact that I had to change positions made the transition even more challenging.

At the time, I was about five feet eleven inches tall, and weighed about one hundred and ninety pounds. I was number four on the depth chart for my position, and it was a long shot for me to play being a freshman. There were two seniors and a junior in front of me on the depth chart competing for playing time. The one secret weapon I had was that big ass chip on my shoulder, and having fought for everything my whole life. On the college level, I was fighting to be seen. Summer camp was fast paced and the coaches came in strategizing and putting in their schemes for the first game. They did not have time to babysit freshman players who were just trying to survive. There is this word that has resurfaced again, and again as you have read this book. That word is consistently, favor. Favor has followed me my entire life!

Because I was not afraid, I started to draw the attention of some of the coaches. I jumped in line multiple times to get extra reps when we did live drills. I got away with it for a couple of weeks until my position coach noticed it while watching practice film. They wanted to know who this freshman was jumping the line and sacrificing his body more than anyone else just to get on the field. Either he was desperate to get on the field or crazy! The truth was wherever I went that little devil who had a voice in my head, went to. He would tell me things like, *"You are not good enough to play on this level. They are going to chew you up and spit you out. Why are you even here?"* As I reflect on those moments, I was battling the summer heat, my teammates, my playbook and that little voice in my head that told me I could not do it.

Through all of my hard work, I somehow found favor with my head coach. I moved up to number two on the depth chart even though I felt like I was playing like number one. There was a senior in front of me, and the Defensive Coordinator worshiped the ground he walked on. Due to me being new to the program my opportunities were limited. I was pressing and doing everything I could to be seen and get on the field. Towards the end of camp I pushed myself to the point I injured myself. I suffered a high ankle sprain three weeks out from my very first college football game. I was so disappointed because I felt like I blew an opportunity even though it was a long shot for me to play anyway.

I remember getting treatment from the trainers one day during practice. I was riding the stationary bike when my head coach walked up. He said, *"How are you doing, Waites?"* I kind of choked up because I didn't even think he knew my name. I told him I was good, and he said *"If you were good, you would not be riding this bike right now."* and laughed. He leaned over, got close and whispered in my ear, *"I need you to be ready to go in a couple of weeks for our first game at South Carolina State."* I almost fell off the bike, but I said, *"Yes, sir."* He looked me straight in my eyes and said *"I believe in you."* Up until that point, no one other than Aunt Ada had spoken with such conviction who firmly believed in me and saw my ability and potential.

I busted my ass to get healthy enough to play even though I was not one hundred percent. I did not get any practice with the first team or even the second team leading up to the game. Most of the practice, I received was from mental reps. Meaning I mentally walked myself through the plays. Game time rolled around and I remember while I was stretching I was really encouraging and hyping my teammates up. I realized that it was bigger than me and my desire to play. Out of nowhere, my head coach walked up to me, grabs me by the face mask, and says *"Don't let me down,"* and walked away. I really did not understand what was happening until I was called to go on the field with the first team defense. I was shocked, excited, afraid, and most importantly I was determined not to let my coach down. This moment caused me to feel the same way I did when my dad told me years ago after walking me to the edge of the football field to *"Just Hit'em Before They Hit You."*

In my first collegiate game, I had three tackles, two pass deflections, and a fumble recovery. Until that day, I struggled to articulate the feeling I felt that hot day in Orangeburg, South Carolina. I was not sure what happened behind the scenes, but there was no turning back. I started the entire year at strong safety as a true freshman, and was awarded at the end of the season with the *"Best Newcomer"* award. The funny thing about favor is that God will intentionally hide you, sometimes even in plain sight, until he is ready to bring you from behind the curtains to the front stage. Sometimes favor doesn't make sense, add up, or to some, favor ain't fair. Looking back, my journey from feeling invisible and struggling academically to finding my place on the football field, and in life highlights the transformative power of perseverance, and faith.

My freshman year brought significant changes, including a budding relationship with Chelice, who I instantly knew would be my wife despite her initial rejection of me. I don't know how I knew, but I just did. I walked into the party thinking I had it going on. I was a freshman football player who actually played. You couldn't tell me I wasn't bigtime, but when I saw her, I felt like I was drowning.

Her beautiful skin instantly made me think about the Egyptian Queen Cleopatra. The way she moved was subtle, elegant, and efficient, not wasting one movement or motion. I built enough courage to walk up and speak to her saying, *"Hello."* She said to me, *"Hey."* I told her my name and asked for her name. She said, *"My name is Chelice."* I thought I was making headway and decided to take the leap and ask her to dance. She said, *"No, I don't think so. I have a boyfriend, and I won't do anything to hurt his feelings."* Even though she shut me down, I was so impressed with the way she handled the situation. It was confirmed to me that at that moment, she would be my wife, so I shared my revelation with her. I told her right then, after being denied a dance, that she would marry me one day. Of course she laughed, but just like in the Chinese proverb, *"He who laughs last, laughs best."* I have been laughing for the past thirty years, and Chelice has been right by my side.

I will not pretend to know how or why I knew it. I just did! It goes back to favor, and how we are chosen for certain things. I was hiding in front of Chelice in plain sight until I wasn't. The great thing about our blooming relationship was we started out as friends and became best friends. Remember, she initially told me she was dating someone, and was not going to do anything to hurt him. Her loyalty and dedication really inspired me, and I respected her for that. I was satisfied with just being almost like a brother to her. We hung out and all of our friends thought something was going on but it was not. I remember trying to hold her hand once, and she looked at me with a *Arnold from Different Strokes* face, as if she was about to say *"What you talking bout Willis?"*

She wasn't having it and she stood on the fact that we could only be friends. I allow myself to believe that I wore her down because at some point she and her boyfriend decided to move on from one another, and our relationship developed. It developed to the point where every waking moment either one of us had was spent together. We went to the movies, skating, basketball games, and pretty much everywhere together. We never talked about it, but we both knew she was starting to realize and believe what I knew from the beginning. It really dawned on me that Chelice loved me when we were both about to go our separate ways at the end of the semester. I was going home to Charleston and she was going to Georgetown, South Carolina. We had a miscommunication. I was going to put fuel in my car for my trip home, but she thought I was leaving without telling her goodbye. As I was leaving, I could see her in my rearview mirror watching me, but I did not understand why. When I returned after getting fuel, Chelice was crying, and I asked her what was wrong. She said *"I thought you left without saying goodbye."* That was the moment I realized she loved me and we were on to something.

## Chapter 6

# FAVOR FOUND ME

> *I embrace the unexpected paths in my journey, trusting favor will guide me to my purpose and extend its blessings beyond myself to enrich those around me.*

When you are favored, favor doesn't just spill or pour on certain parts of your life. It saturates every single part of your being. The crazy thing is when you are favored, the overflow of your favor drips on everyone close to you. Imagine God's blessing showering on you from the heavens, drenching you from the crown of your head to the sole of your feet. The overflow enriches those nearest—your family, friends, and future generations. Yes, favor extends beyond oneself, nurturing those in its vicinity with hope and prosperity. When you are favored, generations depend on your blessings to not only survive but to strive and thrive. I knew when I met Chelice that she and our children were the ones that God chose to catch the overflow of my blessings and his favor.

This truth became evident during my career in law enforcement, a path I had not envisioned for myself, especially coming from communities where the police were often viewed with skepticism. Yet, favor doesn't follow plans; it orchestrates them. I was not a kid who had aspirations of growing up and becoming a law enforcement officer. Growing up in Harlem and then Charleston, I was always afraid of the police. Not because I was doing anything wrong, but because law enforcement did not have a good reputation in my community, and the only time I saw them was when something bad happened. Besides, the idea of becoming any type of professional as an adult was off the table for me because I thought of myself as a nobody who would never evolve into being somebody.

My unexpected journey into law enforcement began while serving in the Army in 1995, amid a family crisis with my father's health. The rapid response from my military family to get me stateside after relaying the message from the Red Cross my father was not well was my first tangible experience of favor in action. The military hop, though uncomfortable, was a blessing. I was serving in the United States Army at the time, and it was a challenge getting a flight out of Ramstein Air Base to Charleston.

A hop is a military operational flight that has extra seats. Whatever the military is transporting takes priority over extra seats any service members may occupy. I remember like yesterday being excited to be able to get on the hop with my wife and my daughter Jasmin, who was almost two years old at the time. Little did we know we would spend eighteen hours sitting with our backs to the wall on a C130 cargo plane. It was one of, if not, the most uncomfortable plane rides I had ever experienced. Luckily, Jasmin spent most of those eighteen hours sleeping.

We made it to the Charleston Air Force Base, after a twenty-four-hour layover in Delaware. We went straight to the hospital to check on my dad. We learned of the rare condition he had that made his organs appear on an x-ray as if you were looking at a mirror. His organs being flipped around in his body did not cooperate with the hospital's technology, and though his heart issues were serious, the strange readings made his condition seem worse than it really was. After spending time checking on my dad and making sure he was alright, my family and I split time between Charleston and Georgetown, South Carolina, where my in-laws resided. Jasmin was a bundle of joy at the time, and both sides of the family wanted to get their hands on her. We planned to be stateside for thirty days, so everyone would have ample facetime with the newest grandchild to the family. When we stayed in Georgetown, I was bored out of my mind because I was still getting to know Chelice's family and really didn't know anyone. It was there, amidst the slow pace of small-town life, I had a transformative encounter.

My brother in law, Isaac L. Pyatt Sr. held a leadership position at the local Sheriff's Office and seemed to be down to earth and a good person to his core. Besides, his name was Isaac just like my dad, so he had to be *good people*. Right? I remember one day, he stopped by my in-law's house in his squad car and said *"Let's ride."* He was the first law enforcement officer I really came in contact with, and had an opportunity to get to know. He said, *"I stopped by to save you because I know the last thing you want to do is sit around here all day."* He was absolutely right.

That day Isaac gave me a personal tour of Georgetown County, which was a hidden gem tucked away in between Charleston and Myrtle Beach. The diverse communities and beautiful countryside really caught my attention. For a little while, I forgot about my dad's health issues, and was really just enjoying the day. However, an emergency call of service for Isaac was broadcast over his squad car radio. He looked at me and said, *"For your safety, I have to drop you off at my office."* He dropped me off at an office building that appeared to be in the downtown historic district of Georgetown. I found myself waiting in the sheriff's office, an invisible observer to the comings and goings of local law enforcement.

I sat there for about an hour watching people come and go. Some officers walked in with people in handcuffs, did paperwork, and just sat in there to take a quick break. The odd thing was nobody ever spoke to me or acknowledged my presence. It almost seemed like I was invisible. All of a sudden, an older Caucasian man walked in the back door. He was short, kind of stoudt, soft spoken, and kind of looked like someone's uncle. It was here Sheriff Cribb acknowledged me. He said, *"Hey young man, how are you?"* I replied, *"I am well."* He asked, *"Who are you here to see?"* He wanted to know whether someone was helping me. I told him what happened with Isaac and he said, *"Come on back to my office. I'm Sheriff Cribb, Isaac told me about you, and I'm pleased to meet you."*

For the next two hours, our conversation detailed various topics, from family, to my military role, to the essence of law enforcement. The Sheriff was intrigued with the idea I was in the military intelligence field, and the fact I was a Morse Interceptor copying Morse code from countries who were not friendly to the United States. I was intrigued by what the Sheriff had to say about law enforcement. I asked him, *"What do you love about being a law enforcement officer in general?"* His answer was simple but profound. He told me that he liked helping people. I also asked him what he disliked about the profession, and he told me he never got used to telling a parent their child was gone. Sheriff Cribb's passion for helping people, and his candid reflections on the challenges of the job resonated with me, offering a new perspective on a profession I had once viewed from afar. We talked and laughed and I was so astonished by how friendly, whitty, kind, and intelligent Sheriff Cribb was. Our meeting concluded, and Isaac returned. Sheriff Cribb's parting words unknowingly laid the groundwork for my future: "If you ever need a job and I'm still the Sheriff, give me a call." In that moment, unbeknownst to me, favor had found me, setting the stage for a career that would intertwine with my purpose and identity. Favor is not just about the individual, but about how one's blessings can brighten the paths of those around us, ensuring the impact of favor is felt across generations.

Chapter 7

# SWIMMING WITH THE CURRENT PURPOSE AND SERVICE

*I am strategically placed in my journey, empowered to make a meaningful difference, and aligned with my purpose. I move forward with confidence and impact.*

The anxiety of potentially losing my father before reaching Charleston was an experience I vowed never to relive. After deliberate contemplation, prayer, and weighing the pros and cons, I was honorably discharged from the U.S. Army in June 1997. My family resettled in my wife's hometown of Georgetown, South Carolina, where we embarked on a new life after my military career. It was in Georgetown that I began a new journey in law enforcement, realizing I was not just called, but chosen.

Sheriff Cribb, a man true to his word, hired me at the Georgetown County Sheriff's Office. I underwent eight challenging weeks at the South Carolina Criminal Justice Academy in Columbia, South Carolina. There were physical challenges I met during my time at the academy, but was no problem due to my past experiences as a college athlete and a veteran. My absence from my family was the hardest part. However, it was at the academy where I met lifelong friends, Eric

Watson and Kevin Riley, who helped keep me focused and out of trouble. Eric Watson was a quiet man and was assigned as my roommate. He currently serves as the Deputy County Administrator for Charleston County, in South Carolina. Kevin Riley was just as rowdy as I was, and works today for the United States Marshal Service in their training division. The three Amigos, as we were once called, created a bond that still flourishes today. After completing the academy, I returned to Georgetown to begin my career as a certified law enforcement officer.

I will never forget my mother's first comments when I shared the news I was joining the ranks of law enforcement. I was never one to consult with many people upon making major decisions. I depended on God to guide me, so when I told my mother the decision had already been made. Her initial response was *"Out of the frying pan, back in the fire."* In other words, she was saying I was going from one bad situation to an even worse one. To a certain degree, she was right. Of course, I was a soldier in the U.S. Army, and I was at risk, but becoming a certified police officer put me on the front lines of dealing with the forces of evil every day.

I really enjoyed law enforcement early on for the wrong reason. I believed my sole purpose in this noble profession was to arrest the *"bad guy."* I soon fell victim to the frustration of arresting the same bad guys over and over. That frustration grew when I was exposed to arresting the sons, nephews, and brothers of the bad guys who I initially arrested. It was a nasty cycle that needed to be broken, especially in the minority communities across my jurisdiction. I saw up close and personal the negative impacts of violence, drug-distribution, drug-use, and drug-addiction on a daily basis, and it was not a pretty picture. I remember thinking to myself *"Did I really sign up for this?"* The process of only arresting the bad guy was more complicated than I anticipated.

I expressed these concerns to Sheriff Cribb, telling him I felt we could do more for the community, especially the youth. He acknowledged my efforts in keeping dangerous individuals off the streets, but understood my frustration with the ongoing cycle of crime. He said, *"You should be proud of the work that you've done so far."* He was right, but I couldn't get that nasty cycle out of my head which ultimately turned into a heavy burden. I had an overwhelming desire to make a difference and not just arrest people. I wanted to find a way to work with the community to break the cycles that were destroying it.

I received a call from Genola Williams, who questioned our efforts in drug education. I remember her asking, *"Who is in charge of the drug-program for your organization?"* I answered proudly, *"I am."* She said *"Good, I'm talking to the right person."* I was not prepared to answer the next question she asked me. Mrs. Williams asked with conviction, *"What are you doing to educate young people about the dangers of drugs in Georgetown County?"* Ashamed, I admitted our focus had been narrowly on enforcement. She quickly said in a higher pitched voice, *"That is not what I asked you; I asked you what are you doing to educate young people about the dangers of drugs in Georgetown County?"* I was ashamed but I answered Mrs. Williams by simply saying *"Nothing, Mrs. Williams."* She said, *"Well, I want to meet with you,"* and she invited me to lunch at the local Elk's Lodge where she was a distinguished member.

Contrary to her formidable phone presence, Mrs. Williams was a petite, elegant woman in person. She sounded really tough over the phone, reminding me of one of my Drill Sergeants when I attended Basic Training at Fort Jackson, South Carolina. Over lunch, she emphasized the importance of early drug education. From that day moving forward, we became great friends and this meeting led to the organization of the community's first *Red Ribbon Parade and Festival*, a successful event that combined fun and education, with activities like a petting zoo and speakers like Robert Geathers Jr., who was a local professional football player during that time. It took a lot of teamwork to get it done, but it was a success. While the kids were having fun, we educated them and their parents about the consequences of drug abuse such as the effects on their health, and how drugs could prevent them from achieving their goals and dreams. That day I truly understood what service was all about, and I felt like I had purpose.

Watching the festival, Assistant Sheriff Weaver complimented the initiative, and I was deeply moved, realizing how impactful my role could be. As a couple thousand kids ran around amplifying roars of joy, he looked at me and said, *"You did this, and this is awesome."* I literally fought back tears because I was truly overwhelmed. Even though my life started one way, things were changing for the better. It's remarkable how purpose fuels you—like swimming with the current or having the wind propel you forward. I felt fulfilled, knowing I was making a meaningful difference, not just passing through life but leaving a lasting impact. This was a clear instance of being in the right place at the right time to answer Mrs. Williams' call. Once again *"Favor found me,"* to help me realize that I was strategically put here for a purpose. I was starting to learn my role in God's Production.

## Chapter 8

# WHY ME?

*I embrace my role in touching lives, knowing each interaction carries the potential to plant seeds of hope and transformation.*

My career continued to evolve. While deeply entrenched in my law enforcement career as a Narcotics Investigator, I faced the daunting challenge of tackling drug-addiction, abuse, and the illegal sale and distribution of drugs in my jurisdiction. As the leader of a multi-jurisdictional drug task force targeting mid to high-level drug organizations, the job was perilous, complex, and time-consuming. Yet, I was passionate about my role because it felt like I was making a meaningful contribution.

I was blessed to have a dedicated group of men and women whom I worked with towards this monstrous effort. My commitment required long hours, often at the expense of family time. I remember nights when I'd come home at four or five in the morning after intense surveillance, missing the morning routines of my wife and children. This demanding schedule persisted for weeks, taxing not only myself ,but also my family, who endured nights of uncertainty about my safety.

One memorable case involved the arrest of a young man I'll call Tony to protect his identity. His arrest was unlike any other; he wept uncontrollably, which was unusual compared to other detainees. It was clear there was something deeper affecting him. During the arrest, a colleague harshly criticized him for his actions, but I felt this was unfair. I remember my co-worker telling Tony, *"You are a dope dealer; What are you crying for? I bet you wasn't crying when you were selling this poison to people in the community."* Even though we had evidence that Tony was a drug trafficker, and was heavily involved in the *"drug game,"* I still felt like my co-worker's comments were too harsh. Tony was still a human being, someone's child who had made mistakes.

To spare Tony further distress, I volunteered to transport him to the detention center. As I drove down the road, I continued to look in my rearview mirror, and I observed a human being who seemed as if he was defeated with no way of turning things around. It was almost like he felt like he was in last place. *Does that ring a bell?* As Tony continued to weep, I finally said, "Hey man, everythings gonna be alright."

His response to me was: *"Nah man, you just don't understand. Number one, I knew it was only a matter of time before y'all came for me because I turned my back and walked away from God, and got myself caught up in this game. Number two, I was scheduled to preach my trial sermon in less than six months, and become ordained as a minister. I have thrown it all away."*

I was like *WOW*, this is really crazy, but I believed every word Tony said because he said it with such conviction. I could see and feel his pain and disappointment. After about three minutes of silence which seemed like thirty minutes, I said to Tony, *"If God intended for you to preach His Word, then you will preach His Word."* I went on to tell him, *"If you ever get your life back on track, and you are about to preach that trial sermon, let me know because I might just come and check you out."* Once we arrived at the detention center, I booked Tony in and left. Before I left the detention center, Tony thanked me, but I doubted I would ever see him again, given the severity of his charges.

Eighteen years later, as the Police Chief of the Georgetown Police Department, I received a message from someone named Tony. My Administrative Assistant gave me a few notes of phone calls I missed and needed to return. I made a few calls, and the missed call from Tony was the last one I returned. Once I made the call, a gentleman with a raspy voice answered. I said, *"Hey Tony, this is Chief Waites, and I'm returning your call. I'm sorry I missed you earlier. How can I help you?"* The gentleman said *"Hey Mr. Ke(l)vin. How are you doing?"* Someone calling me Mr. Ke(l)vin made me believe that this was someone who I dealt with back in the day, but the name did not register with me. In his raspy voice, with a slight Gullah Geechee accent, he asked if I remembered him. I told him that the name sounded familiar to me, but I could not place him.

Tony replied by saying *"Let me tell you a story."* He said *"About eighteen years ago, I was arrested on drug trafficking charges, and I was sentenced to twenty years in prison."* He told me God blessed him in that he only had to serve twelve years before being released on parole. I was listening, but I still couldn't figure out who I was talking to. He said *"The day I was arrested, I told you that I was scheduled to preach my trial sermon."* Boom, just like that, it all came back and I got it. He said *"You told me that if God wanted me to preach his word, I would, and if I was ever in a position to preach my trial sermon to let you know. Well, I'm preaching my trial sermon this Saturday and I'm calling to invite you."* I was speechless and didn't know what to say or how to feel. Although I knew I was going, I told Tony I would have to check my schedule. He understood and gave me the location and the time of the service. I knew I was going because I was in search of something. Sometimes when you work in an industry where you see so much bad and negative things, it becomes easy to fall into a black hole. You become cynical without seeing any hope on the horizon. The call from Tony gave me hope, and even if my schedule was full that day, nothing would have kept me away from attending Tony's trial sermon.

The service started at eleven Saturday morning, but of course the police officer in me made me arrive at the church at about ten-twenty to watch people as they showed up. It was awesome to see all of the people who came out to support Tony on this day. There were close to two hundred people in attendance. I slipped in the back of the church at about ten-fifty, with just enough time to slip in unnoticed to sit on the back row. The service leading up to the sermon was really good with singing, and the reading of Bible scriptures. I recognized Tony as soon as he walked in with the other pastors to take their respectable seats in the pulpit area. I thought to myself when I saw him *"He does not walk like how he walked back in the day, and quickly referenced our phone conversation, realizing he did not talk like he did back in the day either."* Something was different. It was obvious to me what was different about Tony was God's anointing on his life.

The time had come for Tony to step up to the microphone and deliver, and *deliver* is exactly what he did. I remember the name of his sermon like it was yesterday. The topic was *"Broken, But Not Forgotten."* He preached about the prodigal son, and eventually how he came back home. At one point, our eyes connected and he thanked me for being there, saying in front of the entire church I saved his life. *What a roller coaster ride! What a whirlwind!* I remember thinking he had close to twenty years to practice this sermon and he nailed it. After the service, I went and spoke to him and he immediately embraced me and started crying saying, *"Thank you so much."* My response was *"No, I thank you today because you gave me something I was in search of. You gave me HOPE and I'm so happy for you."* At a time, when all I saw was murder, drugs, and rape, Tony pulled me up out of that black hole and reminded me I was on an assignment. He reminded me that just like him, I too, was favored. Even when it seemed like we both were in last place at a certain point in our lives, God turned it around and helped us to realize we were not just called but we were chosen. I often wondered, *"Why was I the one to transport Tony to jail that day? Why did I encourage him not believing I would ever see him again? Why did Tony find me to invite me to be a part of one of the most important days of his life? Why did I go?"* Reflecting on why I was the one to transport Tony that day, and why he reached out to invite me, I realized we impact every life we touch. Tony's story rekindled my faith in the power of redemption and the deep-seated purpose of my work. The key takeaway from my experience with Tony is profound: we leave a legacy with every interaction. What kind of legacies are you crafting with the lives you touch?

## Chapter 9

# FOR A TIME SUCH AS THIS

*I am chosen for my unique role and purpose, equipped to lead with integrity and impact, transforming challenges into opportunities for unity and positive change.*

Throughout my extensive law enforcement career, I was blessed with many opportunities to learn what true service really means. I graduated from prestigious programs like the DEA's Drug Unit Commander's Academy, and the FBI National Academy at Quantico, Virginia—opportunities that many in my field never experienced. I was blessed to have trained with law enforcement executives from across the globe. My roommate, for the ten months I spent at the F.B.I. Academy was from the country of Uganda.

There were a lot of ups and downs during my career; however, I can truly say the good always outweighed the bad. The last sentence in Matthew 20:16 states that "Many are called, but few are chosen." In other words, we are all called and invited by God to follow him and receive his Salvation, but very few of us accept that invitation, and are then chosen to do a great work. Being chosen doesn't mean that you get special treatment and you are untouchable. *"Chosen"* from my experiences, and perspective means that you will *"serve,"* even when nobody is patting you on the back or thanking you. It means that you will *"serve,"* when you know your enemy means you no good. Ultimately, you will *"serve"* when it hurts, is uncomfortable, or potentially may even cost you your life. Many things during my twenty plus years in law enforcement allowed me to understand I was called to this noble profession, but a few things happened to make me realize I was not only called, but I was chosen. The funny thing about being chosen is God will hide you for a *"time such as this."*

Despite the ups and downs, the positives of my career always outweighed the negatives. Matthew 20:16 says, "Many are called, but few are chosen." This resonated with me, highlighting that being chosen to serve is not about receiving accolades or escaping harm, but about serving faithfully under any circumstances, even when it's painful, uncomfortable, or life-threatening. I have learned that we should not serve for personal gain, but we should serve so that God in some form or fashion gets the Glory.

In June 2016, a pivotal moment came: I was appointed the first African-American Police Chief of Georgetown, South Carolina, the third oldest city in South Carolina which was founded in 1729, and a city enriched by its history tied to indigo and rice, cultivated originally by African slaves. Before this, I was the Interim Chief at the Horry County Police Department, one of the largest and fastest-growing counties in the country. A call about the Georgetown position presented a significant crossroad.

Horry County offered a chance to lead a large department with ample resources to support the needs of the community and a higher salary. I was at a fork in the road, and it was one of the toughest decisions that I had to make during my law enforcement career. In addition to this, there was a substantial difference in the pay of both organizations. Taking the job in Georgetown would cause me to leave several thousands of dollars in salary on the table. However, Georgetown offered something invaluable—the chance to impact the community that shaped me. Having a direct impact on the community was a big deal for me.

This decision kept me awake for nights, which turned into weeks, wrestling with the choice I had in front of me. While my wife Chelice was supportive, she always kept it in between the lines by saying *"I got your back either way."* One night as I tossed and turned around 3:30 am, a thought came to me in the form of a question. I call it a thought but I knew it was God. The question was, *"Why haven't you prayed and asked me what to do?"* I immediately started praying, asking God for guidance and wisdom to help me make a decision that would benefit my family and I, as well as the community. A decision that would allow me to work in my purpose, and do the most good.

A few days later a divine intervention came in a dream, guiding me toward Georgetown. I dreamed I got up just like I did every morning, got ready for work, and backed out of my driveway in the squad car I was assigned by the Horry County Police Department. While I was on my way to work, I did not make it to the end of my road before my tan colored Chevy Tahoe stalled out and cut off. I popped the hood and got out of the vehicle to take a look. I did not see any issues or problems under the hood that stood out to me. The dream continued by me walking to the back of the vehicle and just standing there for a moment looking at it. Suddenly, the ground under the right side of the Tahoe gave way, crumbled, and the right side of the vehicle fell into a large ditch. I immediately woke up from the dream knowing it was some type of sign.

I met with Georgetown's Mayor Jack Scoville, who expressed a commitment to diversity and community representation. Mayor Scoville was a tall above middle aged white man with a very deep but distinctive Southern accent. He was an Attorney by trade, and was well known, and liked by the entire community. People respected him, thought of him as fair, and he was approachable. If you hung around the Historic District of Georgetown long enough, there was a possibility you would see Mayor Scoville walking the streets with his dog. During our meeting, he said, *"Kelvin, it's time for us to do a better job of representing the entire community, and you are the man for the job."* He asked me to think about it, and let him know my decision as soon as I could.

My conversation with Mayor Scoville that day cemented my decision to serve where my career began. In August 2016, I officially became the Police Chief. I remember the County Administrator from Horry County's reaction when I made him aware of my decision. He said, *"Kelvin, they can't pay you like we can."* I remember saying respectfully in that moment, *"It's not about the money."* I knew that God opened the door, and I was destined to serve the people of Georgetown, South Carolina. The population of the City of Georgetown was close to ten thousand people at the time and predominantly African-American. The thought of Georgetown being founded in 1729, and it taking two hundred and eighty-seven years to hire its first African-American Police Chief humbled me. I was often reminded of the historical significance as I walked through the Historic District past the Rice Museum, which is also the town clock, knowing that at one time slave auctions were held in that same building.

I will never forget the day I was officially sworn because it was truly a bittersweet day for me. So many thoughts ran through my mind as I laid in bed all night the night before praying, meditating, and looking at the ceiling. I did not sleep a blink that night. I say bittersweet but let's start with the bitter. The bitter for me was Isaac Waites was not there to share that moment with me. Although he was not physically there, I thanked him knowing he was smiling from above. It bestowed joy upon me as I reflected on him for always being positive even though he had every reason to be bitter about life, and for always encouraging and letting me know that the sky was the only limit I would have in life. The sweetness of the moment was that my praying mother, Frances Waites was able to see and experience this moment with me. She was able to hold the Bible while I was being sworn in. We often debated the *"calling"* that we both knew God put on my life. She believed that my calling was to be a pastor preaching the Gospel of Jesus Christ. I always countered my mother's theory with the fact I believed law enforcement was my ministry. It turned out at least for the moment, I was right. I looked at law enforcement as my ministry because God directed my path, and ordered my steps during the entire journey.

While being sworn in, I promised my colleagues I would bring one hundred percent to work every day, and I would also demand the same of them. I talked about how it was our organization's responsibility to keep our citizens safe, and work towards building upon and improving our relationship with the community. Officials from all over the State of South Carolina whom I had the honor and pleasure of working with in the past came out and showed their support. It was truly a special day. Sheriff Cribb, and my brother in law, Judge Isaac L. Pyatt Sr., were both present to wish me well. They both played a major role in my personal life and my law enforcement career. I felt blessed to have my tenure as chief marked by efforts to bridge community divides. During that time, nobody really wanted to openly discuss the division within the community, even though everyone knew there was an elephant in the room. The elephant in the room was the fact that older generations, younger minds, different races, different cultures, and classes struggled to co-exist. Instead of doing the hard work by having difficult conversations, these issues were glazed over and ignored on a daily basis. On one hand, there were segments of one community who believed I was there for them and only them. On the other hand, portions of another community looked at my hiring as *"There goes the neighborhood."* The real work had just begun.

It was my second week and my administrative assistants called my office to let me know that there was a walk- in up front to see me. I always took the time to speak to the community as they walked in even if they did not have an appointment if my schedule allowed me to do so. She asked if I wanted her to walk them back, but I insisted on going up front to greet them. Once I opened up the door to the lobby, I could not believe what I saw. I saw a fair skinned older black man, in a dark three piece suit, and a crispy white shirt with no tie. His hard black shoes almost blinded me as I quickly glared at his feet. His hair was well groomed and his mustache was perfect, as if it was painted on his face. He was *"cleaner than the board of health."* He reminded me of someone special to me, and that someone was my father, the late Isaac Waites.

I walked the gentleman back to my office, while inquiring whether or not he needed a bottle of water or a cup of coffee. He said, *"No thank you, I'm good right now."* When I got back to my office, I told him that he could have a seat. I did not sit behind my desk to talk with him. Instead, I pulled up a chair close to him to make him feel comfortable. The first thing that came out of his mouth was, *"Son, we are proud of you. I never thought that I would see a black Chief of Police in my lifetime."* I was very humbled by his remarks and thanked him. He told me he stopped by to congratulate and welcome me to the community. As we sat and talked, he invited me to a community event that he was planning. He told me he really wanted to do something for the young people in the community and he asked if I would attend and speak to the kids. My response was *"Absolutely, anything to help and encourage our young people."* He was excited that I would be attending, and said *"Oh yeah, one more thing. Please don't bring any white police officers with you."* His comment caught me off guard and really disappointed me. I responded to the gentleman by saying, *"If that is the case then I nor any of my officers will be participating with your event. I'm here to bring people together not to continue to drive wedges between us."* My encounter with this gentleman in my office, who looked strikingly like my late father, underscored the community's complex dynamics. His initial request for me to exclude white officers from a community event challenged my commitment to unity, which I stood firmly for.

He quickly recanted his statement and told me that it was fine for any officers to come. I respectively told him that due to the fact I knew where his heart was I would not feel comfortable attending the event, but maybe I would attend a different event in the future. Although I was disappointed, there was no way I could compromise myself and attend that particular event.

During another occasion, I was summoned to a wealthy citizen's home to discuss his displeasure with certain individuals and challenges within the community. I listened to the gentleman and offered feedback regarding the situation being firm, fair, and respectful. This citizen had the nerve to ask me at one point if I liked my job, as if they were somehow trying to intimidate or threaten me. There was always some type of moral *"Tug of war"* especially surrounding small town politics; however, I loved serving the community and standing in the gap for people who may not be able to stand up for themselves.

My leadership was further tested during the COVID-19 pandemic, a stark reminder of the unseen dangers we face. The Covid-19 pandemic was a real thing, and I remember lying in bed at night wondering what my organization would do if the entire police department became sick. Providing adequate emergency services was an ongoing commitment to the community while doing our best to limit the exposure of our officers in an attempt to keep everyone healthy. We often trained and prepared for storms, mass shootings, bomb threats, you name it. What we were not ready for was the silent killer that was ravaging our community, and unexpectedly snatching people's loved ones in the middle of the night. It was a very challenging time for my organization, but I believe it made us stronger and more resilient in the end.

Nothing compared to the societal upheaval following the murder of George Floyd. This event shook the world and inevitably our local community. Racial tensions infiltrated every community across the globe after George Floyd was murdered at the hands of a police officer in Minneapolis. I remember sitting in my office watching the footage, and I was in disbelief. I was angry, hurt, and confused at how someone who wore a uniform just like I did could commit such a heinous act. We all watched the reactions of people from various backgrounds, races and ethnicities. Both peaceful and not so peaceful protests took place across the country in major cities as well as across the world. I laid awake at night wondering how my community would respond because being a Police Chief, it was my responsibility to keep all people in my jurisdiction safe. I looked to the north, and I saw the tension and reactions of the community. I looked to the south, and I saw what started out as peaceful protests unexpectedly became ugly. One thing I had never seen in my lifetime was people of different races, cultures, classes, and every walk of life stood up, stood out, and stood together in the name of humanity.

This global event prompted a profound engagement with local NAACP President, Mr. Marvon Neal. When he called, he said, *"Chief, we are marching."* He wanted me to know there would be a large protest, and he invited me to a meeting to speak with the community as they started planning and organizing the event. I went to the meeting not really knowing what to expect. As I sat in the meeting, I could see and feel the pain in the faces of the young and old. I witnessed the anger, frustration, and the desire of the community to impose its will on racism, and a criminal justice system who they did not trust or believe in. I sat and listened until Marvon finally asked, *"What do you think, Chief?"* I explained to the group of about fifty people that I was not there to tell them what to do, but instead I was there to support them, and make sure that they were safe as they exercised their right to have a peaceful protest. I did ask one favor of the group, and that was wherever and whenever they decided to have the peaceful protest, please do it during the day time. There were so many incidents across the country where people had good intentions of having peaceful protests, and people with not so good intentions created havoc while camouflaged under the cover of darkness. The organizers agreed to honor my one request. I felt really blessed to work in a community where law enforcement was trusted enough to be invited to this meeting because nobody had to say anything. It could have been planned, and local law enforcement could have been left in the dark.

There was a lot of planning and resources that went into keeping the protestors as well as the community safe. We partnered with local authorities as well as the state police to make sure we had more than adequate resources to support this event, and prepared for every possible outcome. It was June 6, 2020, and the day had come. Because I was exhausted for obvious reasons, I was not sleeping well. We were expecting two to possibly four thousand people to participate in the protest. We were at the Georgetown Police Department going over our operations plan making sure that everyone was on the same page.

On the day of the protest, a challenging conversation with one of my officers who questioned the relevance of George Floyd's death to our community turned into a crucial teaching moment. The plan was to brief a couple of hours prior to the event, and for the officers to then deploy to their post. At the end of the briefing, right before we hit the street, I asked everyone in attendance, *"If all hearts and minds were clear."* Suddenly, one of my officers stood up and said *"Chief, I'm really struggling* with something." I was surprised because this particular officer never said much. He went on to say that he did not understand why people were marching here in Georgetown because George Floyd was murdered in Minneapolis. He went on to say *"This is not an issue for our community."*

I thanked him for stepping forward and speaking up as I was certain that he was not the only person in the room who felt that way. He just happened to be the one who had enough courage to ask the question. As he was talking, I thought to myself *"wow."* Things were already tense, and the air in the room was thick. After thanking him, I spoke from my heart in answering his question, knowing that I was answering the question for everyone. I started off by acknowledging the officer was correct in that George Floyd was not murdered in Georgetown, South Carolina. Then, I spoke to the group which consisted of police officers from the Georgetown Police Department, State Police, as well as National Guard soldiers. I told the group:

{*"George Floyd was murdered in the living rooms and on the cell phones of people all across the globe, and because of that, many people are traumatized and hurting. Hell, I'm hurting because when I watched the footage of what happened first and foremost, I saw a human being brutally murdered while begging for his mother to help him. He cried out like he knew he was about to die. In addition to that, when I saw Mr. Floyd on the ground with a knee on his neck I saw my father, my uncle, my brother, and I saw my own son. People are sick and tired of being sick and tired, and are crying out for justice. People want to express themselves, and somehow find a way to heal from what we all witnessed. That is why people here today, and all across the globe are marching. They are marching for* healing and justice, and we have an opportunity today to be a part of the healing process while our citizens peacefully protest the brutality that took place on May 25, 2020 in the streets of Minneapolis. In addition to that we have an opportunity today to go out and shine a positive light on an industry that is currently in a dark place. We have an opportunity today to show the world how to protect and work with our community. Will someone call you out of your name today? Probably! Will someone at some point say F the police as you walk by? Maybe! When the community decided that they were going to march, they called and said "Hey, this is what we are doing and we want to include you." That is truly a blessing because we have all watched the news the past week, and seen the violence and destruction that has occurred as a result of Mr. Floyd's death across the country. You do understand that the community did not have to call us, and we could very well be playing catchup, and having to respond after the fact? Again, to answer your question the people of Georgetown and the surrounding areas are marching and peacefully protesting for healing and justice."}

    I explained the impact of such injustices reaches far beyond their immediate locations, affecting humanity universally. Our participation in the march was not just an act of solidarity but a critical step toward community healing. While I had so much more I wanted to say, I cut it short because I felt myself getting emotional, and that was the last thing I needed to do before we hit the streets. For the first time in my life, I could really feel what Dr. Martin Luther King Jr. meant when he said *"Injustice anywhere is a threat to justice everywhere."* I asked if anyone else had any additional questions. You could hear a pin drop in the room, but I heard the officer who asked say *"Thank you,*

*Chief."* At that point, everyone left the law enforcement facility and deployed to their respective posts. As I rode over to the site where the peaceful protest was going to start, I prayed that God would protect the community as a whole, and these moments would transpire into healing and peace.

As I parked my car, a revelation was revealed to me. One that froze me dead in my tracks and would not allow me to get out of my car just yet. I realized at that moment I was not only *"CALLED, but also CHOSEN"* to be the Chief of Police in Georgetown, South Carolina at this time. Not just chosen by Mayor Scoville, or any other politician, but I was *CHOSEN* by God for this specific assignment. A specific moment! This moment! I was chosen to answer the police officer's question about why people were marching and protesting in Georgetown, South Carolina. I realized at that moment that as the first African-American Police Chief for Georgetown, South Carolina, I was destined and equipped with a tool box full of life's experiences, and different perspectives that prepared me for this moment. I do not believe someone else would have been able to answer the officer's question in a manner that would bring peace, resolution, and a reaffirming commitment to the situation. Before I got out of my vehicle, I was so stirred up by the revelation, I said it outloud to myself. *"I was chosen, and God I thank you for this moment."*

As I posted up at the vacant lot where everyone was meeting, I started seeing people who I had not seen in several years. People from all walks of life started showing up. It was the first time I saw people put politics, social status, age, gender, sexual orientation, the color of their skin, and every other indifference aside to choose HUMANITY. Ironically enough, this all took place in a small community called GEORGEtown as a result of GEORGE Floyd. I've never been a person who is a big believer of coincidences because everything happens for a reason. People young and old continued to gather. Before I knew it, close to twenty-five-hundred people showed up ready to express themselves, and help our community start the healing process. I saw people carrying signs that said things like:

*"I have decided to stick with love"*

*"I can't Breathe"*

*"The Color of our Skin is Not a Weapon"*

*"We are Family"*

*"My Future Matters"*

*"Justice for George Floyd"*

*"Breathing is a Human Right"*

The march started, and it was an all around beautiful day. The weather was perfect and everyone was on the same accord. I along with, Brendon Barber who was the Mayor at the time, and Sheriff Carter Weaver from the Georgetown County Sheriff's Office marched with the masses. The protest was a powerful demonstration of unity and empathy, with diverse community members joining in solidarity. It culminated at East Bay Park, where we collectively kneeled for the duration that George Floyd suffered, a poignant reminder of the need for empathy and change.

Reflecting on my role, I recognized being chosen by God for this moment was not just about leading in times of peace, but guiding through turmoil and advocating for justice and humanity. This realization confirmed that my career, while marked by many challenges, was ultimately about serving a greater good, a legacy of empathy and unity in the face of adversity.

## Chapter 10

# NEW SEASON

*I am guided by divine timing and purpose, trusting that each new season brings opportunities for growth and fulfillment aligned with my true calling.*

In May of 2021, I underwent a significant back surgery, a two-level spinal fusion, necessitated by an injury from my time in the United States Army. The prospect of surgery was daunting; I had never been under anesthesia, had heard daunting stories about back surgeries, and had never missed work due to an injury. I managed the pain since leaving the Army in 1997, but it had progressively worsened to a constant presence.

If I was awake, I would be in pain. I hid this from my family for years, but the time had come that I could not hide it anymore, and I had to do something about it. I never complained; I just continued to push through until I couldn't. The decision to finally address it was unavoidable. My doctor assured me that being put to sleep was the least of my worries. My doctor said, *"From the time you go under anesthesia until you wake up, you will be heavily monitored by medical personnel. It would be just like you have airplane pilots monitoring your oxygen, blood pressure, and heart rate. You are going to have the best nap of your life."* He continued to explain I would be out of work for about two months recovering, and once I returned, it would only be on a limited basis until I had fully recovered. My major concern was my daughter was scheduled to graduate from law school, and I wanted to be there, but I could not put this surgery off any longer. I had surgery, and I remember waking up with a group of nurses around me asking questions. They asked if I knew why I was there, and did I know the day of the week. It seemed like I was only out for five minutes, and I was pleasantly surprised by the fact that the surgery had gone well. To my relief, the constant pain and pressure I had been enduring were gone, replaced only by the discomfort of fourteen staples in my back. Recovery was strict and required careful attention to avoid bending or sitting too long, as per my doctor's instructions. My wife, Chelice, was an immense support during this time, diligently reminding me of the post-op care I needed.

This period of forced downtime was new to me, as I was accustomed to always being actively involved, not on the sidelines. It gave me a chance to reflect, read, and reconnect with my family, and appreciate the events I had missed over the years. Although I couldn't attend my daughter, Jasmin's graduation in person, I was grateful to watch it virtually. This slow recovery allowed me to realize just how non-stop and hectic my life had been for more than two decades.

After twenty-seven years of service between the military and police work, I felt like I had done my part. Those two months at home helped me realize there was life after law enforcement for me, and God still had more work for me to do. I wasn't just healing physically because my time at home away from all the noise solidified my decision it was time for a new chapter. Conversations with AMI Kids, an organization dedicated to empowering youth, led me to accept a position as their Executive Director in Georgetown. This role felt like a continuation of my life's work, albeit in a different capacity.

I enjoyed working with the young men in the program as well as the dedicated staff, but my time with AMI Kids was brief, as I felt called to another opportunity. A message about a job opening in Myrtle Beach for a Director of Diversity, Equity, and Inclusion caught my attention. The position aimed to foster an inclusive culture in a town known for its significant tourism despite its small size. The job description resonated deeply with me, reflecting my career experiences and aspirations to create an environment where everyone felt valued.

Myrtle Beach is known across the globe as an historic beach town of about thirty-five-thousand permanent residents. Even though its population is smaller than most major cities, over twenty million people visit Myrtle Beach from across the globe annually. People from different cultures and walks of life visit Myrtle Beach to enjoy the beautiful beaches, fine dining, recreation, and the night life.

The job description outlined how the Director would be responsible for the city's diversity, equity, and inclusion strategy, as well as collaborate with the leadership team members to advance equity as a core component of Myrtle Beach's culture. When I read the job description, it caused me to recall some of the experiences good and bad I encountered early on in my law enforcement career. I promised myself one day I would be in a position to help create a culture, atmosphere, or climate where everyone felt valued, and felt the psychological safety needed to speak their truth. Honestly, when I read the job description I believed somehow it was written just for me. Over the next couple of days, I took my time and filled out the online job application.

The week leading up to my in person interview, I found myself suffering from a severe case of food poisoning. I was not feeling well. I have no idea what I ate, but it caused me to feel sick. I was dehydrated, weak and on top of that I could not keep any food or liquids down. It was really difficult to focus and do the research necessary to be prepared for my upcoming interview. I thought long and hard about calling the city and trying to reschedule. There was no way I could have been at my best in the condition I was in. The day of my interview came, and I was finally able to eat a banana and keep it down. I arrived for my interview, and sat down to speak with a five person panel about the city of Myrtle Beach's new initiative, why I thought it was important, and what I believed I brought to the table. My interview lasted about forty-five minutes, but it seemed more like a conversation than a formal interview. I answered all of the questions to the best of my ability, and then it was my turn to ask any questions I had. I questioned the panel regarding the new initiative, specifically asking if the city was serious, or just wanting to check a box. After I asked the question, four of the five panelists looked at the City Manager simultaneously. The City Manager, Fox Simons reassured me of their sincerity and commitment to change. I left that day feeling good about the process, and even better that I did not get sick, or feel nauseous during the interview.

Once I left City Hall, I could feel the weakness setting back in on me. The timing of it all made me scratch my head and wonder, *"Why is this happening now?"* That entire week, despite my untimely sickness, I asked God to help me focus, gain clarity, and have a breakthrough regarding the opportunity in front of me. Reflecting on that week's challenges, a conversation with my friend, Pastor Deshawn Rouse, provided a profound perspective. He suggested my physical ordeal was akin to an unintentional fast, perhaps a divine intervention to focus my spirit on what lay ahead. He said, *"Kelvin, sometimes God will put you on a fast and not even let you know."* Ultimately, I was offered the position, a role that encapsulated the essence of my career efforts in fostering diversity and equity. Being granted this opportunity, allowed me to confirm God was still ordering my steps.

Starting this new chapter, I felt a strong sense of being exactly where I was meant to be, affirmed by my experiences, and driven by a purpose that had guided me throughout my entire career. It was a powerful reminder that being in alignment with your purpose transcends the immediate struggles, positioning you for future impact and fulfillment. I felt blessed, fortunate, and most importantly FAVORED. It's hard to feel like you are in last place when you know that you are doing what you were called to do.

## Chapter 11

# FIRST

*I am favored and destined for greatness; my journey reflects a powerful legacy of leadership, purpose, and transformative impact.*

In mid-November 2022, while recording an episode of my podcast, "Safe Conversations with Kelvin Waites," I engaged in a profound dialogue with my daughter, Jasmin Waites Parker, then a Prosecutor for the State of South Carolina. "Safe Conversations" was created as a platform to foster courageous discussions on critical social issues like racism, antisemitism, sexual identity, poverty, and more. This particular episode, featuring Jasmin, centered on her experiences as an African American female attorney in the South. I had recently introduced a segment allowing guests to ask an unscripted final question, often eliciting deep personal reflections. Jasmin's question took me by surprise: "Daddy, I've watched you go hard all your life, serving the community and sacrificing for us, always putting yourself last. Why have you always gone so hard?"

Her question left me momentarily speechless, a rarity. After a pause, I admitted my fear of failure had always driven me. This fear had me "playing not to lose" rather than "playing to win." I shared with Jasmin despite my achievements, I always feared losing what I'd worked so hard to gain. This podcast recording marked a pivotal realization; I had been building self-equity without recognizing its full extent. This new awareness shifted my perspective from playing defensively to actively celebrating my achievements and embracing the future with the knowledge I was not only building value in myself, but also enriching those around me. I still have a lot of gas left in my tank. For the first time in my life, I realized I was really FAVORED, and because of it, I was blessed to go from what I believed to be last to being FIRST.

This shift in outlook reaffirmed my identity as a leader. As the first African American Police Chief in Georgetown, South Carolina—a city whose prosperity was historically extracted from the labor of enslaved Africans—I understood the deep historical and communal significance of my role. I saw pride in the eyes of elders who had survived the Jim Crow era and hope in young people who struggled to see their potential. I prayed that my tenure would transcend my racial identity and instead reflect my commitment to justice and community unity.

When I accepted this role, I prayed that I would not just be known as the first black chief because I did not want it to be a distraction. I prayed that people from all walks of life would look past my skin color, and see the God in me. As a result of this, when I was hired not one media or news outlet mentioned anything about me being the first African American Police Chief of the City of Georgetown. I wanted to be known as one of the best Police Chief that Georgetown ever had. One who cared about the people. Young, old, white, black, gay, or straight, I was chosen to stand in the gap for people who could not stand up for themselves. It was not an easy task at all because I was what I considered black and blue. I was black because there I stood, an

African American man who knew that in the past the police department I was charged to lead had not always been friendly to the minority community. I was blue because I swore an oath to protect and serve. The two worlds sometimes clashed, but God brought me through by giving me the spirit of discernment, and the will to always do the right thing;Even when it hurts.

I became the inaugural Director of Diversity, Equity, and Inclusion for the City of Myrtle Beach, which is one of the fastest growing cities in the nation. While dealing with hate and sometimes even racism, I endured some of life's toughest lessons during my law enforcement career. I made a vow to myself to one day be in a position to make a difference by helping employees know that they matter and have value. By working with my teammates, we are pushing towards creating an atmosphere where people do not have to suffer in silence, but have the space to speak their truth. Working as the DEI Director for the City of Myrtle Beach has afforded me the opportunity of a lifetime. We, as a team, work every day to make things better for everyone. Not just one group of people, but all people within our organization, as well as the community. Myrtle Beach is a special place that welcomes people from all over the world, even during a time when diversity, equity and inclusion is being scrutinized. Diversity, equity, and inclusion is often politicized due to lack of education, understanding and fear. I have a running joke that I share with people as I speak with different groups. I tell them if I ever win the PowerBall, I'm going to rebrand diversity, equity, and inclusion. I will call the rebrand DTRT, which will stand for "Do The Right Thing," because at the end of the day, that is what diversity, equity, and inclusion is all about.

On a personal note, becoming the first person in my family named Kelvin Anthony Waites held significant familial and emotional weight. You are probably thinking, *"What's the big deal about that?"* In 1997, my wife and I named our second child Kelvin Anthony Waites Jr., known affectionately as KJ. He was very respectful to everyone he came in contact with and he had manners, which always made me think about my Aunt Ada. She would always say, *"Ya see Cabin, manners will get you what money can't."* She meant that as a young man, if I was respectful and had manners, it would unlock doors for me that may otherwise stay closed. What she said served me well and those same teachings served KJ. He attended Methodist University in Fayetteville, North Carolina graduating with a Bachelor's Degree in Healthcare Administration. After graduating from college, KJ later married his childhood sweetheart ShaQuiel Goss. We knew ever since middle school that those two were pretty close, and after he finished college and she did a stint in the U.S. Army, we knew it was only a matter of time. They are such a beautiful couple, and we are extremely proud of them. I remember the day they told us they were going to have a baby, and how excited everyone in the entire family was. Months later, I was sitting in the garage one Saturday evening talking to KJ when he told us it was a boy. I would have been happy either way, but there was another boy in the family.

I was on cloud nine, but then KJ and ShaQuiel changed the game even more by deciding to name their son, my grandson, Kelvin Anthony Waites III. They said they would call him Tripp for short. What an incredible honor and blessing, because I realize that this is not a common thing to do these days. They did not have to do it, and I believe this is the greatest honor that I have experienced up until this point in my life. Why was such an honor bestowed upon my name? What did I do to deserve this? What does this say about what kind of father I was to KJ? Why me? The answers to all of these questions and many more were simple and right in front of me my entire life. Reflecting on these milestones, from professional achievements to personal joys, I recognized the full spectrum of my blessings. Being able to hold my grandson and know he carries on our name was a profound honor. Each of these "FIRSTS" was not just a personal victory, but a step towards broader cultural and familial legacies. It reinforced a deep-seated belief that my life's trajectory, from feeling last to becoming first, is a testament to being favored by a force greater than myself. I am *"FAVORED,"* and God took me on a journey from once feeling like I was last, to knowing I am *"FIRST."*

# You Too, Can Be First

In the weave of time, where stories blend,
A whispered truth on winds ascend:
"Though many are called, few are the chosen,"
Echoes softly, a promise unbroken.
From the back of the line, in shadows dim,
Where hopes hang heavy, and chances slim,
There lies a heart that beats unstirred,
Clinging to a sacred, ancient word.
In the quiet corners where the last ones stand,
Grace reaches out with a gentle hand.
It lifts the weary, it rights the wrong,
It sings to the forgotten their victory song.
Remember, the first will be last, the last shall be first,
A divine reversal to quench life's thirst.
For the table is vast where the humble are fed,
Where the meek find honor, and the hungry are led.
So if today finds you trailing behind,
If the light seems lost and hard to find,
Hold fast to faith, let not your spirit sway,
For favored are you, in the grandest way.
The race isn't won by the swift or the strong,
But by the souls who've been faithful all along.
And just when it seems all chances are past,
God's grace whispers, "You're first, not last."

Matthew 20:16

May this poem inspire and uplift those of you who may feel overlooked or last, reminding you that in God's eyes, you hold a place of favor and potential for greatness.

# WORKBOOK

# About Favored From Last To First Workbook

This workbook is designed to be a companion guide, deepening your engagement with Kelvin Waites's powerful memoir. Each activity from crossword puzzles that challenge your recall to affirmations that reinforce the messages of resilience, questions prompting reflection, and journaling spaces for personal insights serves to connect you more intimately with Kelvin's narrative. It invites readers to internalize the Biblical principle from Matthew 20:16—"the last will be first"—which is woven throughout Kelvin's life.

    Engaging with this workbook, readers are encouraged to reflect on their paths, embrace their growth, and see how, like Kelvin, they might apply this scripture's wisdom to overcome their own adversities and rise to new heights. Through these interactive exercises, you will explore the depths of perseverance and the heights of achievement. This workbook is more than just a test of memory; it's an invitation to apply Kelvin's life lessons to your own journey, to discover hope in your story, and to reaffirm that indeed, the last can become first.

## PUZZLE CHAPTER ONE:

**WORD BANK**

Favor, Faith, Fast, Actors, blessings, generations, upbringing, education, hate, situs inversus, veil, eyes, en caul, birth, culture, blessing, protection, prophecy, greatness, Harlem, New York, projects

## SOLUTION

# Week One

## BASED ON CHAPTER ONE

**This Week's Affirmation is:**
I recognize that the journey to success is not found in shortcuts, but in the steadfast climb, step by step, with courage and determination shaping my destiny.

**Reflection:**

*"Being Last"* narrates the challenges and life lessons from growing up in poverty in Harlem, New York. Kelvin and his family lived in a small apartment that he and his brother, Bryan dubbed their *"penthouse,"* highlighting their optimistic perspective despite their stark reality. Their family struggled financially, but strong family bonds and a vivid imagination provided comfort and entertainment. Their grandmother, Viola, in the Bronx added spiritual depth to their lives, teaching them the 23rd Psalm and instilling values through unique bedtime prayers.

Despite hardships like bullying due to physical disabilities and severe asthma, Kelvin learned resilience and hope. The daily uncertainty of their building's elevator working symbolized their constant struggle, turning even a simple journey to their apartment into an ordeal. These experiences were compounded by the violence and crime witnessed daily in Harlem, which deeply impacted their sense of security..

This chapter encapsulates a journey of overcoming adversity through familial love, faith, and a refusal to seek shortcuts, emphasizing that true success requires perseverance, akin to climbing stairs step by step. You too, like Kelvin, can choose to see good when the circumstances in life may be far from the life you desire. You must work daily to change your reality and build the life that you desire, and take steps daily. These steps may be small, but remember that many small steps will equate to one big step. You are in control of shaping your destiny.

**Essential Questions for Development:**

1. How can you cultivate resilience and hope in the face of adversity, drawing inspiration from your experiences?

2. In what ways can you strengthen your family bonds and embrace imagination to find comfort and entertainment in challenging times, similar to the Waites family?

3. How can you instill values and spiritual depth in your life, inspired by Viola's teachings and unique bedtime scriptures and prayers, to navigate hardships with grace and purpose?

## SOLUTION

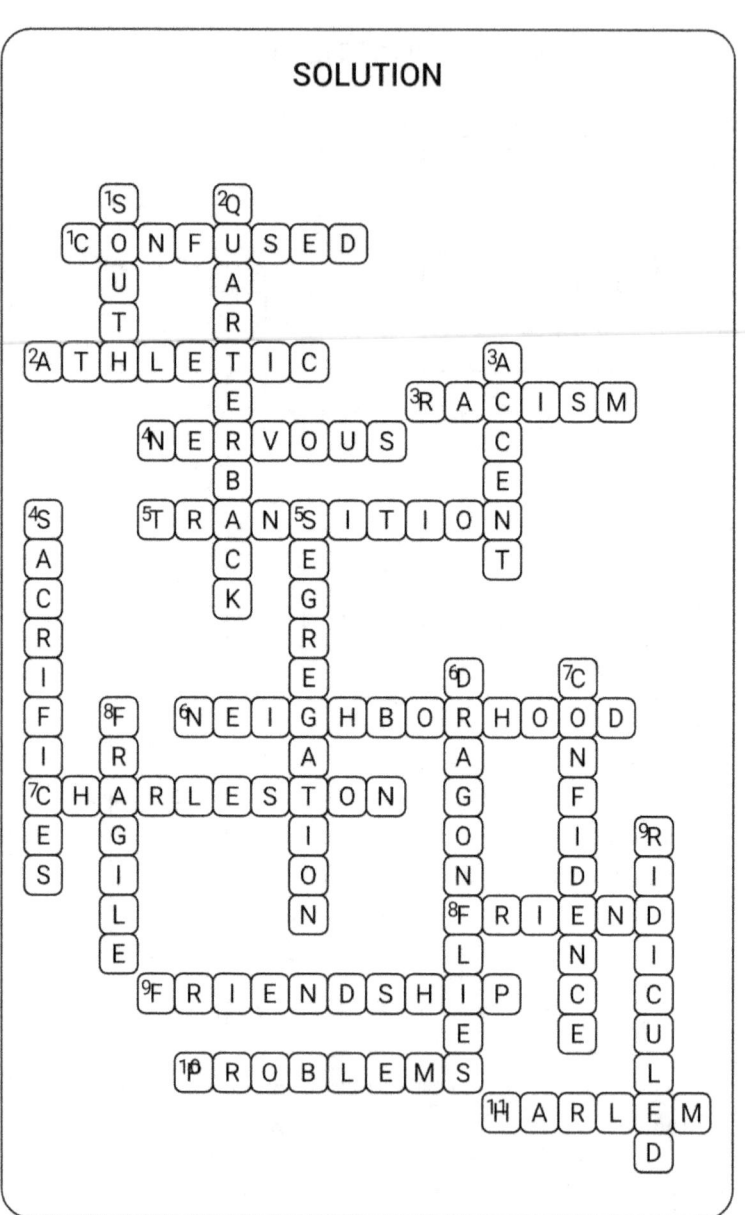

# Week Two

## BASED ON CHAPTER TWO

**This Week's Affirmation is:**
I embrace new beginnings and challenges as opportunities to grow, proving to myself that with resilience and determination, I can adapt and thrive in any environment.

**Reflection:**

Chapter Two, titled, *Get In The Game* describes Kelvin's determination to adjust to life in Charleston, South Carolina. It was in this city where his family hoped for a better life; however, after the move, he faced new challenges. Adjusting to the new environment was tough; his Northern accent and appearance made him a target for ridicule, and he struggled to fit in, managing to make only one friend, John, despite racial tensions. Kelvin was determined not to disappoint his parents as he understood even at an early age that they made great sacrifices to provide a better life for him and his brother.

His parents grappled with employment issues and financial strain, yet they encouraged him to persevere. Kelvin faced internal conflicts, pressured to adapt and succeed to honor his family's sacrifices. Ultimately, he sought to join the local football team as a way to integrate and prove himself. After convincing his parents, he embraced the sport, finding confidence and identity in his athletic ability, spurred on by his father's simple yet powerful advice to tackle challenges head-on, symbolizing a broader life lesson. This chapter teaches us that even when things go wrong, we do not have to go along. Just as Kelvin fought through his hard days, and tough moments, you too, can work through obstacles, and reach your goals.

## Essential Questions for Development:

1. How can you embrace determination and resilience in the face of new challenges, drawing inspiration from Kelvin's experiences in Charleston, South Carolina?

2. In what ways can you navigate internal conflicts and external pressures to adapt and succeed, similar to Kelvin's journey of honoring his family's sacrifices?

3. How can you find confidence and identity in your abilities to integrate into new environments and prove yourself?

# PUZZLE CHAPTER THREE:

**WORD BANK**

Trailing, Football, Imposter, Achievements, Recognition, Isolated, Excellence, Hope, Solace, Heritage, Accent, Believe, Darkness, Revival, Preaching, Weeping, Usher, Touch, Revelation, Savior

## SOLUTION

# Week Three

# BASED ON CHAPTER THREE

**This Week's Affirmation is:**
I recognize my worth and embrace my journey, knowing that my struggles are part of my story, leading me to true strength and resilience.

## Reflection:

After a triumphant football season, Kelvin gained respect from his peers, yet struggled internally with feelings of inadequacy and the harsh reality of popularity. Despite achieving *"Most Valuable Player,"* Kelvin battled the internal voice that labeled him an imposter, unworthy of his successes due to his background and physical challenges. This period was marked by loneliness, even as others suddenly sought his friendship, not understanding the true hardships behind his public victories.

Finding a constructive outlet in sports, he channeled his frustrations into excelling at football, which provided him with a sense of hope and achievement. His friendship with John, though filled with shared experiences, eventually waned as they pursued different paths, emphasizing the transient nature of childhood connections. He often reflected on his Aunt Ada, whose wisdom and deep connection to her Gullah Geechee roots grounded him and instilled a sense of hope and purpose. Her words of wisdom always stuck with him.

The black church played a significant role in his upbringing, mandated by his parents who believed in its importance for moral grounding and facing life's challenges. Despite initial resistance and mischief, a profound experience during a church revival led to a spiritual awakening, accepting faith as a cornerstone for navigating life's trials and tribulations.

**Essential Questions for Development:**

1. How can you overcome feelings of inadequacy and imposter syndrome, drawing inspiration from your struggles and triumphs?

2. In what ways can you find constructive outlets for your frustrations and challenges, to channel your emotions?

3. How can you cultivate deep connections and wisdom from your roots or community to ground yourself and find purpose?

## PUZZLE CHAPTER FOUR:

**WORD BANK**

Journey, Faith, Struggle, Teenage, Belief, Courage, Conviction, Awakening, Blessing, Problems, Persona, Transparent, Dreams, Procession, Funeral, Casket, Terrified, Revelation, Anointing, Responsibility

## SOLUTION

# Week Four

## BASED ON CHAPTER FOUR

**This Week's Affirmation is:**
I trust in the journey and embrace my unique path, knowing that each challenge I face is a divine opportunity to strengthen my faith and demonstrate resilience.

**Reflection:**

In this chapter titled, *"New Level New Devil,"* Kelvin grapples with the complexities of adolescence and faith after his spiritual awakening. Despite his newfound commitment to Christianity, Kelvin struggled with openly expressing his faith, and he often felt embarrassed among his peers to say that he is a Christian. Kelvin expresses that he felt torn between maintaining a tough persona among peers and a devout one at home.

Kelvin faced internal doubts about his worthiness of God's love, given his personal challenges. These struggles were intensified by peculiar, prophetic dreams that seemed to foretell real events, adding a sense of divine responsibility that felt overwhelming. His mother reassured him that these visions were a special gift and part of God's plan, which he reluctantly accepted.

Over time, Kelvin realized that these experiences were not just burdens but part of building *"faith equity,"* teaching him that God's past help was a sign of continual support. This realization helped him to face new challenges with resilience, viewing each as a step towards greater spiritual maturity.

## Essential Questions for Development:

1. How can you reconcile your faith with the pressures of adolescence and peer expectations, drawing inspiration from your struggles and growth?

2. In what ways can you overcome internal doubts about your worthiness and embrace the concept of *"faith equity,"* to find strength and resilience in your spiritual journey?

3. How can you balance maintaining a tough persona with openly expressing your faith to live authentically and honor your beliefs?

## PUZZLE CHAPTER FIVE:

**WORD BANK**

Academic, Performance, Football, Middle, School, Invisible, Aspirations, Empower, Career, Parents, Struggles, Support, Survival, Harlem, Belonging, Introvert, Isolation, Confidence, Recruiters, Opportunity

## SOLUTION

# Week Five

## BASED ON CHAPTER FIVE

**This Week's Affirmation is:**
I trust that my unique talents and genuine self will guide me to my rightful place, and I embrace each step of my journey with confidence and faith in my eventual success.

## Reflection

In this chapter *"In Plain Sight,"* Kelvin reflects on his journey from struggling academically and feeling invisible during his school years to finding recognition and self-worth through football. Like so many of us have experienced or will experience, sports became a positive outlet for Kelvin. Football offered him a place to excel and channel his frustrations while reciprocating-building meaningful relationships and learning lessons on the field that became life-long.

Kelvin's skill on the field began to attract college recruiters. Eventually, his talents led to an offer from Newberry College, where he continued to prove his athletic prowess despite initial challenges and a significant injury. His freshman year was transformative, not just in sports but also in his personal life, as he began a relationship with Chelice, whom he confidently believed he would marry despite her initial rejection. This story of growth and overcoming adversity highlights the importance of perseverance and faith, teaching that sometimes, your abilities and potential can be hidden in plain sight, only to be revealed when the time is right. The narrative culminates in the realization of personal strength and the beginning of a lifelong partnership.

**Essential Questions for Development:**

1. How can you identify and nurture your talents and potential, drawing inspiration and finding recognition and self-worth through your life?

2. In what ways can you cultivate perseverance and faith, as demonstrated by your resilience in overcoming challenges and pursuing your goals, even in the face of rejection?

3. How can you recognize the transformative power of relationships and personal growth, to find strength and purpose in your own life?

## PUZZLE CHAPTER SIX:

**WORD BANK**

Journey, Favor, Blessings, Purpose, Generations, Enrich, Skepticism, Overflow, Family, Career, Law, Enforcement, Military, Hop, Hospital, Condition, Health, Leadership, Community, Sheriff

## SOLUTION

# Week Six

## BASED ON CHAPTER SIX

> **This Week's Affirmation is:**
> I embrace the unexpected paths in my journey, trusting that favor will guide me to my purpose and extend its blessings beyond myself to enrich those around me.

**Reflection:**

In this chapter, *"Favor Found Me,"* Kelvin's unexpected journey into law enforcement, a career he had never envisioned due to his negative perceptions of police from his childhood experiences in Harlem and Charleston. His path shifted during a military stint when an urgent family crisis brought him stateside, leading to a transformative encounter with law enforcement through his brother-in-law, Isaac, in Georgetown, South Carolina. This experience, along with insightful conversations with Sheriff Cribb, reshaped Kelvin's views on the police force, showing him the human and helpful side of the profession. The sheriff's invitation to consider a future in law enforcement if ever needed marked a pivotal moment of favor that would later define his career path.

This chapter reflects on how favor does not just enrich the individual but extends its benefits to those around them, impacting family, friends, and future generations. At times, we may not understand how a crisis, big or small, can potentially lead us to a bigger blessing (one that maybe in hindsight). As you reflect on your life, be sure to be in a place mentally- where you are able to receive favor. For example, if an unwanted situation happens, do not get so sad that you cannot cope. Cope with the circumstance, and know that your future is much brighter than your present. Allow favor to find you because you are destined to be first and not last.

**Essential Questions for Development:**

1. How can you reassess and potentially shift your perceptions or preconceived notions regarding law enforcement or people in general?

2. In what ways can you recognize and embrace moments of favor and blessings, even in challenging or unexpected circumstances?

3. How can you cultivate a mindset that allows you to be open to receiving favor and blessings, trusting that challenges may lead to greater opportunities and blessings in the future, as exemplified by Kelvin's journey?

**WORD BANK**

Strategically, Empowered, Meaningful, Difference, Aligned, Purpose, Confidence, Impact, Anxiety, Discharged, Journey, Law, Enforcement, Academy, Physical, Challenges, Absence, Friends, Bond, Frustration

## SOLUTION

# Week Seven

## BASED ON CHAPTER SEVEN

**This Week's Affirmation is:**
I am strategically placed in my journey, empowered to make a meaningful difference, and aligned with my purpose. I move forward with confidence and impact.

## Reflection

This chapter, *"Swimming With The Current: Purpose And Service"* chronicles Kelvin's transition from military life to law enforcement in Georgetown, South Carolina. After an honorable discharge from the U.S. Army, he joins the local sheriff's office, motivated by an offer from Sheriff Cribb. His journey at the South Carolina Criminal Justice Academy is tough but rewarding, fostering lasting friendships and setting the stage for his career. Early in his role, he enjoyed the action of law enforcement but soon became disillusioned by the cyclical nature of crime in his community.

A pivotal conversation with Genola Williams leads him to reconsider his approach, emphasizing drug education over enforcement. This shift results in the organization of Georgetown County's first *Red Ribbon Parade and Festival*, a community event that educates about drug dangers while engaging local youth in positive activities. The success of the event reaffirms his sense of purpose and shows him the profound impact he can have on his community. This episode in his life underscores the theme that aligning with one's purpose feels like *"swimming with the current,"* as efforts align with personal values and community needs, amplifying the positive impact one can make.

## Essential Questions for Development:

1. How can you align your actions with your purpose and values, drawing inspiration from Kelvin's shift towards drug education and community engagement in law enforcement?

_____
_____
_____
_____
_____

2. In what ways can you find fulfillment and a sense of "swimming with the current" in your endeavors?

_____
_____
_____
_____
_____

3. How can you foster lasting friendships and meaningful connections to support your personal and professional growth?

_____
_____
_____
_____
_____

# PUZZLE CHAPTER EIGHT:

**WORD BANK**

Embrace, Interaction, Transformation, Evolve, Investigator, Distribution, Organizations, Perilous, Surveillance, Commitment, Remember, Detention, Minister, Conviction, Ordained, Administrative, Preach, Parole, Invite, Redemption

# Week Eight

# BASED ON CHAPTER EIGHT

**This Week's Affirmation is:**
I embrace my role in touching lives, knowing that each interaction carries the potential to plant seeds of hope and transformation.

## Reflection:

This chapter, *"Why Me?"* reflects on Kelvin's career in law enforcement, particularly his time as a Narcotics Investigator where he dealt with the pervasive issue of drug trafficking. Engaged deeply in a task force, his work was challenging and often came at the expense of family time. During one arrest, Kelvin encountered Tony, a young man caught in the drug trade who unexpectedly immediately expressed regrets about his life choices, including a derailed path to become a minister. Moved by Tony's distress, Kelvin offered words of hope and encouragement during their transport. Many years later, Tony, having served time and changed his life, contacted Kelvin, now a Police Chief, to invite him to his trial sermon.

Attending the sermon, Kelvin was profoundly moved by Tony's message and transformation, reminding him of the potential for redemption and the positive impact law enforcement can have beyond just arrests. The story culminates in a reflection on the meaningful, lasting influence one can have through seemingly routine interactions, highlighting the legacy we leave in every life we touch.

1. How can you recognize and embrace the potential for positive impact in your interactions, to have a lasting influence on others?

2. In what ways can you balance the demands of your work or responsibilities with the importance of family and personal time?

3. How can you cultivate a mindset of redemption and transformation to see the potential for growth and change in yourself and others?

# PUZZLE CHAPTER NINE:

**WORD BANK**

Unique, Purpose, Integrity, Impact, Challenges, Opportunities, Unity, Change, Law, Service, Prestigious, Career, Salvation, Chosen, Serve, Commander, Community, History, Experience, Diversity

## SOLUTION

```
¹S A L V A T ¹¹I O N
          N
          T
²E X P E R I E N ²C E
          G     O
    ³C A R E E R M
          I     M
    ⁴I M P A C T   ⁵L A W   ³C         ⁴C
          Y     A     H   ⁵P         H
                N     A   R         O
                D     L   E         S
          ⁶C    E     L   ⁶S E R V E N
    ⁷C    ⁷O P P O R T U N I T I E S
    H     M   S     G     G
    A     M       ⁸S E R V I C E
  ⁹U N I Q U E   ⁸P     S     O
    G     N     U           ¹⁰U N I T Y
    E   ¹⁰D I V E R S I T Y   S
          T     P
          Y     O
              ¹¹H I S T O R Y
                E
```

130 | Kelvin A. Waites, Sr.

# Week Nine

## BASED ON CHAPTER NINE

**This Week's Affirmation is:**
I am chosen for my unique role and purpose, equipped to lead with integrity and impact, transforming challenges into opportunities for unity and positive change.

**Reflection:**

Chapter nine is titled, *"For A Time Such As This,"* and chronicles Kelvin's reflections on his career trajectory and significant moments that underscored his sense of purpose and calling within law enforcement. After graduating from top law enforcement programs and serving in various capacities, Kelvin faced a pivotal decision between two leadership positions. This chapter details that Kelvin's career has been based on services; he served God; he served his country, and he served his community. As exemplified through his life, we become most great when we serve. Like Kelvin, your life's greater purpose and goals should be aligned with service. For example, you may ask yourself, *"What can I give to others? How can I share? What is a problem that I can contribute to resolving?"* These are questions that will help you to become first if you feel you are last, or if you want to live a more meaningful life.

Kelvin chose to serve, and he chose to serve as the first African American Police Chief in Georgetown, South Carolina, influenced by a divine insight that confirmed his path was not about monetary gain but about impactful service. His tenure as chief was marked by challenging but crucial engagements with the community, particularly during the racial tensions following George Floyd's murder. He navigated these challenges by fostering dialogue and advocating for unity and justice, reinforcing his belief that he was not only called but chosen for such times. This chapter encapsulates Kelvin's journey of recognizing and embracing his role in shaping a more empathetic and united community response to injustice.

**Essential Questions for Development:**

1. How can you align your career and life trajectory with service and impactful leadership?

2. In what ways can you navigate challenging moments and decisions during racial tensions, by fostering dialogue and advocating for unity and justice?

3. How can you recognize and embrace your unique role and purpose, understanding that your actions can transform challenges into opportunities for positive change and unity?

# PUZZLE CHAPTER TEN:

**WORD BANK**

Divine, Surgery, Trusting, Fulfillment, Season, Anesthesia, Army, Doctor, Recovery, Family, Reflect, Military, Director, Equity, Inclusion, Myrtle, Tourism, Job, Interview, Pastor

# SOLUTION

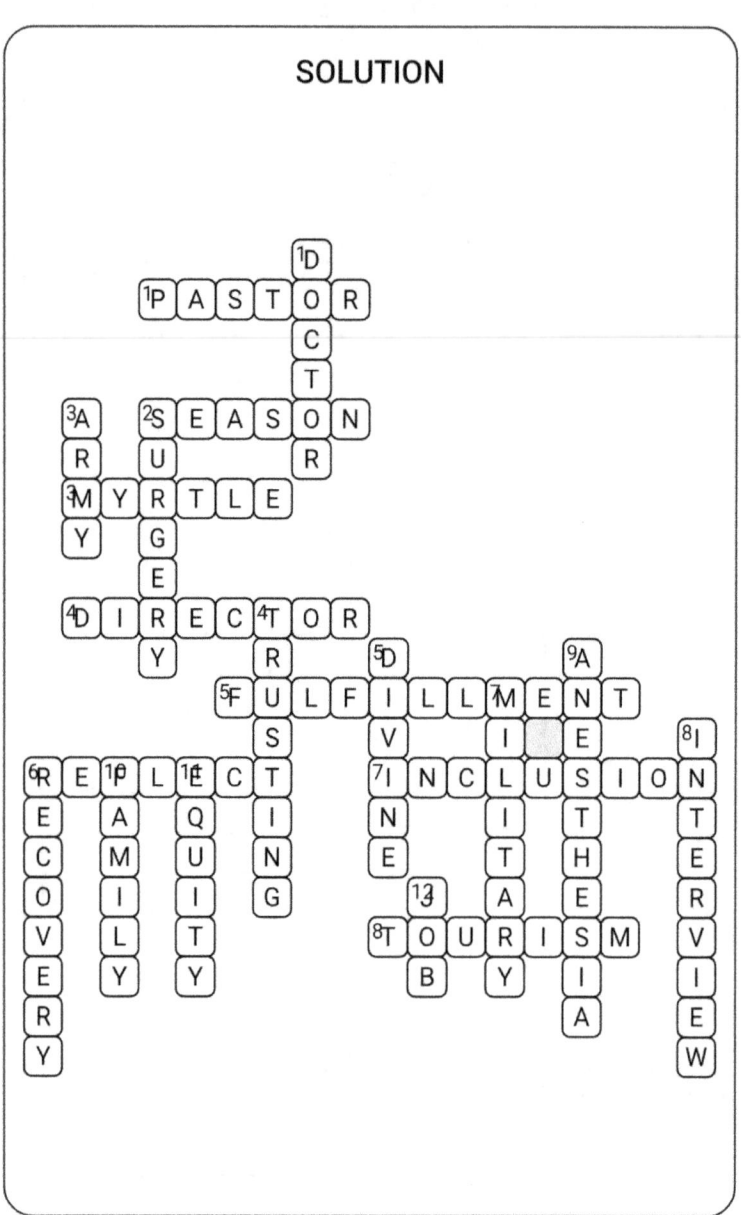

# Week Ten

## BASED ON CHAPTER TEN

**This Week's Affirmation is:**
I am guided by divine timing and purpose, trusting that each new season brings opportunities for growth and fulfillment aligned with my true calling.

**Reflection:**

In this chapter titled, *"New Season,"* Kelvin's transition into a new phase of life following a major back surgery that prompted reflection and reassessment of his life. After enduring years of managing pain from a military injury, the successful surgery offered him a necessary pause, during which he contemplated his long service in law enforcement. This period of recovery not only allowed him to heal physically, but also to reevaluate his journey of life thus far. Ultimately, it led to his decision to retire from the police force and transition into a new role.

Later, called to another opportunity, Kelvin applied for a position as Director of Diversity, Equity, and Inclusion in Myrtle Beach. This opportunity seemed tailor-made for him, aiming to create an inclusive culture in a diverse community. Despite a challenging experience of food poisoning before his job interview, he managed to convey his vision and commitment, securing the position. This chapter reflects on the transformative power of aligning personal hardships and professional transitions with a deeper sense of purpose, emphasizing the serendipitous timing and divine guidance.

1. How can you embrace periods of reflection in your life drawing inspiration from painful experiences?

2. In what ways can you align personal hardships and professional transitions with a deeper sense of purpose?

3. How can you trust in divine timing and purpose, recognizing that each new season brings opportunities for growth and fulfillment aligned with your true calling and purpose?

## PUZZLE CHAPTER ELEVEN:

**WORD BANK**

Favored, Greatness, Legacy, Leadership, Purpose, Impact, Podcast, Dialogue, Prosecutor, Equity, Inclusion, Georgetown, Diversity, Community, Justice, Perspective, Achievement, Blessing, Milestone, Victory

## SOLUTION

# Week Eleven

## BASED ON CHAPTER ELEVEN

**This Week's Affirmation is:**
I am favored and destined for greatness; my journey reflects a powerful legacy of leadership, purpose, and transformative impact.

**Reflection:**

In the chapter titled, *"First,"* Kelvin explores the motivations behind his tireless dedication to community service, prompted by a question asked from his daughter, Jasmin, during a podcast recording. He reveals that his fear of failure and a mindset of *"playing not to lose"* had long driven him. This conversation sparks a significant shift in Kelvin's self-perception, from focusing on defensive strategies to actively celebrating his accomplishments and embracing a future filled with potential. He then discusses his historic role as the first African American Police Chief in Georgetown, South Carolina, emphasizing his desire to be recognized for his effectiveness rather than his race. Kelvin's narrative continues with his role as the Director of Diversity, Equity, and Inclusion for Myrtle Beach, focusing on creating inclusive environments within the community. He shares a personal story about his family, reflecting on the honor of having his grandson named after him, which symbolizes the continuation of his legacy. This chapter underscores Kelvin's journey from self-doubt to recognition of his blessings and the affirmation that he is *"FAVORED,"* viewing his life's trajectory as a testament.

**Essential Questions for Development:**

1. How can you shift your mindset from *"playing not to lose"* to actively celebrating your accomplishments and embracing your potential?

2. In what ways can you strive for recognition based on your effectiveness and impact, rather than external factors like race or appearance?

3. How can you create a legacy of leadership, purpose, and transformative impact in your community and beyond, reflecting on the honor of having your actions and values carried forward by future generations?

# PUZZLE CHAPTER TWELVE:

**WORD BANK**

Whispered, Weave, Hope, Heavy, Clinging, Victory, Honor, Trailing, Favored, Grandest, First, Last, Divine, Quench, Inspire, Hold, Matthew, Gentle, Hand, Thirst, Hungry, Spirit, Swift, Strong, Faithful

## SOLUTION

# Week Twelve

# BASED ON POEM
# YOU TOO, CAN BE FIRST

**This Week's Affirmation is:**

*I am favored by grace, destined to rise from the last to the first, embodying the promise that perseverance and faith leads to divine elevation and victory.*

**Reflection:**

The poem *"You Too, Can Be First"* conveys a message of hope and encouragement to those who feel overlooked or trailing behind in life. It speaks of a divine promise that even though many are called, few are chosen, emphasizing that those who are often last in the world's eyes may be first in God's plan. The poem reminds us to hold fast to faith, and not to lose heart, for God's grace can lead them to unexpected victories and honor. It encourages humility and perseverance, highlighting that true success is not measured by worldly standards, but by faithfulness and steadfastness. The poem concludes with a reference to Matthew 20:16, reiterating that God's grace can transform our circumstances and elevate us to positions of greatness.

## Questions for Development:

1. How can you hold fast to faith and remain steadfast in your beliefs, even when you feel like you're trailing behind or overlooked?

2. In what ways can you embody humility and meekness, trusting in the promise that the last shall be first in God's plan?

3. How can you find strength and encouragement in the belief that God's grace can lead to unexpected victories and honor, even when it seems like all chances are past?

www.ingramcontent.com/pod-product-compliance
Lightning Source LLC
Chambersburg PA
CBHW070105080526
44586CB00013B/1194